Comedy Scenes for Student Actors

Short sketches for young performers

Laurie Allen

MERIWETHER PUBLISHING LTD.
Colorado Springs, Colorado

Meriwether Publishing Ltd., Publisher
PO Box 7710
Colorado Springs, CO 80933-7710

www.meriwether.com

Editor: Arthur L. Zapel
Assistant editor: Amy Hammelev
Cover design: Jan Melvin

© Copyright MMIX Meriwether Publishing Ltd.
Printed in the United States of America
First Edition

Library of Congress Cataloging-in-Publication Data

Allen, Laurie, 1962-
  Comedy scenes for student actors : short sketches for young performers /
  by Laurie Allen — 1st ed.
    p. cm.
  ISBN 978-1-56608-159-7
  1. Young adult drama, American. 2. Middle school students—Drama. I. Title.
PS3601.L4324C66 2007
812'.6--dc22
                        2008041734

          1   2   3   08   09   10

Dedication

To my daughters, Brooke and Melanie

Table of Contents

1. Picture Day

CAST: (2M, 5F) MADISON, MR. DOBBS, JADE,
LAURA, BECKY, MONA, PHILLIP
PROPS: Chair, mirror.

1   *(At rise MADISON rushes to the chair, sits down, and smiles.)*
2   **MADISON: Ready!**
3   **MR. DOBBS:** *(Enters.)* **Great! Let's get started. First, if you would**
4   **turn just your shoulders to the siiiide.** *(Adjusts her*
5   *shoulders.)* **Yes, that's it. Chin down.** *(Moves her head*
6   *down.)* **And tilt your head like this.** *(Moves her head to the*
7   *side.)* **That's it. Now, sit up straight.** *(Steps back.)* **And hold**
8   **iiiit.** *(Moves back as he speaks.)* **Hold it, hold iiiit.**
9   **MADISON:** *(Moves out of the position.)* **Wait!**
10   **MR. DOBBS: What's wrong?**
11   **MADISON: What about my hair?**
12   **MR. DOBBS: Would you like to check the mirror?**
13   **MADISON: Yes, please.**
14   **MR. DOBBS: There's a mirror right over there.**
15   **MADISON: Thank you.** *(Looks into the mirror and arranges her*
16   *hair.)* **OK. I'm ready now.**
17   **MR. DOBBS: All right. Shoulders to the side. Chin down. Head**
18   **tilted. Just a bit more, please.**
19   **MADISON: You know ... I don't like tilting my head to the side**
20   **like this. It feels awkward.**
21   **MR. DOBBS: It helps to erase shadows. A bit more to the side,**
22   **please.**
23   **MADISON:** *(Moves her head.)* **Well, I don't want shadows.**
24   **MR. DOBBS: Yes, that's more natural.**
25   **MADISON:** *(With her head tilted awkwardly, she speaks in a stiff*
26   *tone.)* **Are you sure this looks natural?**

1   **MR. DOBBS: Sit up straight!**

2   **MADISON: I don't think I can sit up any straighter!**

3   **MR. DOBBS:** *(Claps his hands.)* **Come on, come on! Sit up tall**

4   **and straight! That will help reduce the appearance of your**

5   **double chin.**

6   **MADISON: I have a double chin?**

7   **MR. DOBBS: Pictures can be quite revealing.** *(Moves her hair.)*

8   **And one more adjustment right here.** *(Steps back.)* **Now**

9   **hold it ...** *(Quickly steps back as he is speaking)* **Hold it, hold**

10   **it ...**

11 **MADISON:** *(Moves out of the position.)* **Wait! Can we try**

12   **something different? Like this?** *(Looking over her shoulder*

13   *and smiling)* **Isn't this cute?**

14 **MR. DOBBS:** *(Frustrated)* **Miss ... ?**

15 **MADISON: Riley.**

16 **MR. DOBBS: Miss Riley, this is a school picture, not an actor's**

17   **headshot!** *(Takes a deep breath.)* **All right, let's try this**

18   **again.** *(Adjusts her.)* **Shoulders to the side ... Chin down ...**

19   **Head tilted ... Sit up straight ... And hold it ... hold it ...**

20   *(Quickly steps back)* **Smile!**

21 **MADISON:** *(Frowning)* **Wait!** *(Moves out of position.)*

22 **MR. DOBBS: What now?**

23 **MADISON: It feels all wrong!**

24 **MR. DOBBS: Well, it would help if you would smile!**

25 **MADISON: But every year my yearbook picture always turns**

26   **out so bad! And this year I want it to be good! So can't I do**

27   **something else? Maybe this?** *(Makes a dramatic pose and*

28   *smiles.)* **Or this?** *(Poses and smiles.)*

29 **MR. DOBBS: No, you may not.**

30 **MADISON: Or this?** *(Makes another dramatic pose.)*

31 **MR. DOBBS:** *(Begins to adjust her again.)* **Shoulders to the side ...**

32 **MADISON: Wait! Can't I sit like this?**

33 **MR. DOBBS: No! To the side, please! Chin down ...**

34 **MADISON: But I don't like my chin down! And if I have a**

35   **double chin, this isn't going to help!**

1   MR. DOBBS: Head tilted ...

2   MADISON: And tilting my head makes me look all spastic!

3   MR. DOBBS: And sit up straight.

4   MADISON: *(Stiffly)* I feel stupid!

5   MR. DOBBS: *(Steps back.)* Smile!

6   MADISON: *(Not moving, but glaring at him)* What if I refuse to

7   smile?

8   MR. DOBBS: Then, Miss Riley, you will look dumb in the school

9   yearbook. *(Steps back.)* Smile!

10 MADISON: *(Moves out of position.)* Wait!

11 MR. DOBBS: *(Extremely frustrated)* Miss Riley, do you realize

12   how many pictures I have to take today?

13 MADISON: Hundreds?

14 MR. DOBBS: That's right! Hundreds! And I can't seem to get

15   even one picture taken!

16 MADISON: I'm sorry, Mr. ... ?

17 MR. DOBBS: Dobbs. Mr. Dobbs.

18 MADISON: I'm sorry, Mr. Dobbs, but this picture is a lifelong

19   memory for me! One day I'll be all old and wrinkled,

20   sitting around with my grandchildren, showing them

21   pictures of how attractive their granny used to look, and ...

22 MR. DOBBS: Wow. You really think ahead, don't you?

23 MADISON: And Mr. Dobbs, I want my grandchildren to see me

24   for who I am!

25 MR. DOBBS: Which is?

26 MADISON: Dazzling! Unique! Gorgeous! I want my

27   grandchildren to scroll through the rows and rows of

28   pictures and without hesitation be able to say, "Grandma,

29   is that you? Why, you were the cutest girl in the whole

30   yearbook!"

31 MR. DOBBS: So let's take a cute picture!

32 MADISON: Thank you! *(Poses and smiles.)* Ready!

33 MR. DOBBS: *(Dryly)* Shoulders to the side. Chin down. Head

34   tilted. Sit up straight. And smile.

35 MADISON: *(Frowning at him)* But ...

1   MR. DOBBS: Thank you. Next.

2   MADISON: Wait! You took my picture like that?

3   MR. DOBBS: Next!

4   LAURA: *(Enters)* I guess I'm next.

5   MADISON: Wait! Wait! I wasn't even smiling!

6   MR. DOBBS: You had your chance, Miss Riley. If you would,

7   please move out of the way and let this young lady sit

8   down. What's your name, Sweetheart?

9   LAURA: Laura.

10 MADISON: But I was glaring at you! I wasn't smiling!

11 MR. DOBBS: And I told you to smile, didn't I?

12 LAURA: Why didn't you smile?

13 MADISON: Because I wanted to take a cute picture!

14 MR. DOBBS: And you had your chance. Now, if you would get

15   up and let this young lady sit down...

16 MADISON: *(Not moving)* Had my chance? How could I have

17   taken a cute picture looking like this? *(Demonstrates)* My

18   body twisted to the side in an awkward position, my chin

19   to the floor, my head flopped over like some spastic

20   person! And you want me to smile like this?

21 MR. DOBBS: Miss Riley, will you please let the next person sit

22   down?

23 MADISON: No!

24 MR. DOBBS: No?

25 MADISON: Take it again!

26 MR. DOBBS: Miss Riley, retakes will be taken after the first of

27   the year.

28 MADISON: After the first of the year?

29 MR. DOBBS: That's correct. So, if you don't like your picture ...

30 MADISON: This is just great! All my friends will be exchanging

31   pictures and I'll be stuffing them in my backpack! My

32   mom will be all excited to see them and then scream in

33   horror. Mr. Dobbs, please! Please!

34 MR. DOBBS: Do I need to send you to the principal's office?

35 MADISON: You can't send me to the principal's office! You're

1   just the picture guy!
2   MR. DOBBS: I'll be right back.
3   MADISON: *(Jumps up.)* All right, all right, all right! I'm leaving!
4   Happy?
5   MR. DOBBS: I don't think you want me to answer that.
6   MADISON: *(As she exits)* I can't believe this! All I wanted to do
7   was take a cute picture!
8   MR. DOBBS: *(To Laura)* All right, if you would just take a seat.
9   LAURA: *(Sitting down)* I don't really like having my picture
10 taken.
11 MR. DOBBS: I understand. Now, if you would just turn your
12 shoulders to the side.
13 LAURA: Like this?
14 MR. DOBBS: Good. Chin down. And tilt your head to the side.
15 That's it. And sit up as straight as you can. Good. And hold
16 it ... hold it ... *(Steps back.)* Smile! *(Returns)* Good. Thank
17 you. Next! *(LAURA exits. JADE enters.)* If you'll just have a
18 seat right there.
19 JADE: I hate picture day!
20 MR. DOBBS: I understand. Now, if you would just turn your
21 shoulders to the side.
22 JADE: Whatever.
23 MR. DOBBS: Good. Chin down. And tilt your head to the side.
24 JADE: Can you like, hurry?
25 MR. DOBBS: That's good.
26 JADE: Do you want me to say cheese?
27 MR. DOBBS: If you'd like.
28 JADE: Cheese!
29 MR. DOBBS: Let's wait until I step back to take the picture.
30 JADE: Whatever.
31 MR. DOBBS: Sit up straight. *(Steps back.)* And hold it, hold it ...
32 JADE: Do you want me to say cheese now?
33 MR. DOBBS: Smile!
34 JADE: I thought I was going to say cheese!
35 MR. DOBBS: *(Frustrated, he approaches her.)* Do you want to say

1   cheese or smile?

2   JADE: Well, I thought I was supposed to say cheese!

3   MR. DOBBS: Then say cheese!

4   JADE: Cheese!

5   MR. DOBBS: But don't say cheese until I take the picture!

6   JADE: OK, fine!

7   MR. DOBBS: *(Steps back.)* Say cheese!

8   JADE: Do you want me to say cheese and then smile or just say

9   cheese?

10 MR. DOBBS: Smile!

11 JADE: Or did you want me to smile and then say cheese?

12 MR. DOBBS: *(Screams.)* ***Say cheese and smile!***

13 JADE: Cheese! *(Gives a big smile, then stands and exits.)*

14 MR. DOBBS: *Next!* *(Moves about shaking his head and wiping his*

15   *forehead.)*

16 BECKY: *(Enters.)* You want me to sit down?

17 MR. DOBBS: Please.

18 BECKY: I think taking pictures is stupid!

19 MR. DOBBS: If you would turn your shoulders to the side,

20   please.

21 BECKY: *(Turns.)* It's just a way for you guys to make money.

22   Send us home with these dumb looking pictures that our

23   parents feel guilty about not buying.

24 MR. DOBBS: Chin down.

25 BECKY: My mom always buys the entire package even when

26   they're bad. And they're *always* bad.

27 MR. DOBBS: Tilt your head to the side, please.

28 BECKY: Sends pictures to my grandparents, aunts, uncles,

29   cousins ... And you know, I really wish she wouldn't. Like,

30   yuck!

31 MR. DOBBS: And sit up straight.

32 BECKY: And the only good thing about picture day ...

33 MR. DOBBS: Smile!

34 BECKY: Is getting out of class. *(Smiles.)*

35 MR. DOBBS: Next!

1 BECKY: And you know, maybe I'll take my sweet time walking
2 back to math class. You know, smell the roses. Stop in the
3 bathroom. Stop by my locker. Take an early lunch ...
4 MR. DOBBS: Thank you. You may leave now. *(BECKY exits.)*
5 Next!
6 MONA: *(Enters. Enthusiastically)* Hi!
7 MR. DOBBS: Hi. If you would please take a seat.
8 MONA: Oh, sure! Thank you! I bet you love your job, don't you?
9 MR. DOBBS: Yeah, sure.
10 MONA: I mean, you get to meet so many people every day! And
11 make people smile all the time! I bet it's the best job in the
12 world!
13 MR. DOBBS: If you would, turn your shoulders to the side.
14 MONA: Absolutely! I just love having my picture taken!
15 MR. DOBBS: Chin down.
16 MONA: Chin is down!
17 MR. DOBBS: And tilt your head to the side just a bit.
18 MONA: How's this?
19 MR. DOBBS: That's fine. And sit up straight.
20 MONA: Straight as a board!
21 MR. DOBBS: *(Steps back.)* Smile.
22 MONA: *(Gives a huge smile.)* Oh, I just love having my picture
23 taken! Hey, do you want to take it one more time in case I
24 blinked?
25 MR. DOBBS: Retakes are after the first of the year.
26 MONA: Oh, OK! Well, thank you! Thank you so much! *(Shaking*
27 *his hand)* And it was such a pleasure to meet you! I guess
28 I'll see you next year! That is, unless I have to come back
29 for retakes. But I don't think I will. I think they will be OK.
30 OK, well I better go so you can get back to work! Have a
31 great day! And I know you will because you have a great
32 job! Bye! *(Exits.)*
33 MR. DOBBS: Next! *(MADISON rushes in and sits down.)* Oh, no!
34 Not you again!
35 MADISON: Shoulders to the side. Chin down. Head tilted. Sit

1   **up straight.** *(She smiles.)*

2   **MR. DOBBS: Retakes are after the first of the year.**

3   **MADISON:** *(Still smiling)* **Just pretend I'm someone else, OK?**

4   **MR. DOBBS: That's not possible.**

5   **MADISON:** *(Smiling)* **Or pretend I'm not here. Either way.**

6   **MR. DOBBS: We already took your picture.**

7   **MADISON:** *(Smiling)* **One more time, OK?**

8   **MR. DOBBS: Look, this is supposed to go quick!** *(Snaps.)*

9   **Students sit down, I give instructions, they smile, I snap**

10   **and they leave! And after four hundred or so pictures,**

11   **then I get to go home!** *(Looks at his watch.)* **And the way**

12   **this is going today, I'll have to come back tomorrow! And**

13   **the only time that has happened to me was in 1998 when**

14   **an unexpected fire drill sent kids marching out of the**

15   **school. And believe me, I don't like coming back for a**

16   **second day!**

17 **MADISON:** *(Smiling)* **I'll be quick. As soon as you take my**

18   **picture, I'm out of here!**

19 **MR. DOBBS: Next!**

20 **MADISON:** *(Smiling)* **Just take it real quick, OK?**

21 **MR. DOBBS: Next!**

22 **MADISON:** *(Smiling)* **It'll be our secret, OK? I slipped in and you**

23   **didn't notice that you took my picture twice.**

24 **MR. DOBBS: Oh, I noticed! Believe me, I noticed!**

25 **MADISON: I'm smiling! I'm ready!**

26 **MR. DOBBS: Next!**

27 **PHILLIP:** *(Enters.)* **I'm next.**

28 **MR. DOBBS: Good. If you would please take a seat.**

29 **PHILLIP: I would, but ... .** *(Motioning to MADISON)*

30 **MR. DOBBS: Miss Riley!**

31 **MADISON:** *(To PHILLIP)* **Just give us a minute, OK?**

32 **MR. DOBBS: Sir, if you would sit down.**

33 **PHILLIP: I would, but ...**

34 **MADISON:** *(Smiling)* **One quick picture and I'm out of here!**

35 **PHILLIP: Could you please hurry up? I have to get back to gym.**

1   Coach is going over some critical plays for the game on
2   Friday.
3   MADISON: *(Smiling)* I'm ready!
4   MR. DOBBS: *(Takes a deep breath, then steps back.)* Smile!
5   MADISON: I'm smiling!
6   MR. DOBBS: And there we go. Thank you. You may leave now.
7   MADISON: But you didn't take my picture! The flash didn't
8   even go off!
9   MR. DOBBS: Well, what do you know? Sorry about that. Retakes
10   are after the first of the year.
11   MADISON: But I want my retake now!
12   MR. DOBBS: What you want and what you get are two different
13   things, Missy!
14   MADISON: Oh my gosh! How hard is it to take a stupid picture?
15   MR. DOBBS: Obviously not very hard because that's exactly
16   what we took of you!
17   MADISON: What?
18   PHILLIP: Uh ... can we do mine now?
19   MADISON: No!
20   MR. DOBBS: Yes! Sit down!
21   PHILLIP: I would, but ...
22   MADISON: And I'm not budging until you take my picture
23   again! And not another fake one, Mr. Dobbs! A real
24   picture! *(Smiles.)* I'm smiling! I'm ready!
25   PHILLIP: Should I come back?
26   MADISON: Yes!
27   MR. DOBBS: No!
28   PHILLIP: Yes? No?
29   MR. DOBBS: Please, take a seat!
30   PHILLIP: I would, but ...
31   MADISON: I'm not budging, Mr. Dobbs! Shoulders to the side,
32   chin down, head tilted and sitting up straight! Ready!
33   PHILLIP: I'll come back.
34   MR. DOBBS: Don't you dare leave!
35   MADISON: Don't worry. I'm not.

1   **PHILLIP: Me or her?**

2   **MR. DOBBS: She leaves! You stay! Now, take a seat!**

3   **PHILLIP: Again, I would, but ... I don't think she's budging.**

4   **MADISON: I'm not!**

5   **MR. DOBBS: Fine! Fine, fine, fine, fine, fine! One more picture**

6   **of you, Miss Riley!**

7   **MADISON: Thank you.**

8   **MR. DOBBS: Shoulders to the side. Chin down. Head tilted. Sit**

9   **up straight. And hold it ...** *(Steps back.)* **Smile!**

10 **MADISON:** *(Quickly moves into a dramatic pose and smiles. After*

11   *the picture is taken, she jumps up.)* **Yes!**

12 **MR. DOBBS: I told you not to do that! The school pictures are**

13   **all supposed to look the same!**

14 **MADISON:** *(Smiling)* **Oops. Sorry.**

15 **MR. DOBBS: Sit down! We're doing it again!**

16 **MADISON: No! I liked that pose! It'll be cute.**

17 **MR. DOBBS: Sit down!**

18 **MADISON: No!** *(Starts off.)*

19 **MR. DOBBS:** *(Follows her.)* **Come back here! We're going to take**

20   **another picture of you! Then another and another and**

21   **another if that's what it takes! You will look like the rest of**

22   **your classmates!**

23 **MADISON: But I don't want to look like the rest of my**

24   **classmates! I want to look cute!** *(MADISON and MR. DOBBS*

25   *exit as PHILLIP is left standing there. After a moment, he sits*

26   *down in the chair, looks around, and then smiles.)*

2. Lost

CAST: (1M, 3F) MRS. MILLS, RYAN, CASSIE, JANIE
PROPS: Map, schedule.
SETTING: Classroom.

1   *(At rise MRS. MILLS is teaching class as RYAN rushes into the*
2   *room. CASSIE and JANIE are seated at their desks. Other*
3   *students at desks are optional.)*
4   **MRS. MILLS: Correlative conjunctions are used to draw a**
5   **correlation between elements in a sentence. They bring**
6   **different things together and they work in pairs. For**
7   **example ...**
8   **RYAN:** *(Enters.)* **I know, I know, I know!**
9   **MRS. MILLS:** *(Looks at watch.)* **Mr. Hodges, this is the third day**
10 **in a row that you've been late to class.**
11 **RYAN: I know!**
12 **MRS. MILLS: First day of school, I could understand. Second**
13 **day, OK, you're still finding your way around. But today ... ?**
14 **RYAN: OK, so I was coming from the science wing and I took a**
15 **right at the gym, left at the choir room, then another right**
16 **at the cafeteria, but then I just stopped and looked**
17 **around. I thought, am I supposed to go to the right or to**
18 **the left? Right or left? So I took a right.**
19 **MRS. MILLS: That was wrong.**
20 **RYAN: I know that now.**
21 **MRS. MILLS: Mr. Hodges, did you not receive a school map on**
22 **the first day of school?**
23 **RYAN:** *(Pulls out a large map.)* **I have it right here. But it's still**
24 **confusing!**
25 **MRS. MILLS: Hogwash. Anyone with any common sense can**
26 **look at a map and find their way around.** *(Takes map.)* **How**

1   hard is this? A Hall, B Hall, C Hall ...

2   RYAN: D Hall. E Hall. F, G, H, I, J, K, L, M, N ... There's a hundred
3   freaking halls in this school! I mean, in elementary, there
4   were like four halls, plus the cafeteria and the gym. But
5   this ... *(Waves map.)* Look, Z-14! I have a math class in Hall
6   Z-14. Room 240, I think. But I haven't even made it in
7   there yet!

8   MRS. MILLS: You've never been to your math class? Where
9   have you been going?

10   RYAN: Roaming the halls looking for Z-14!

11   MRS. MILLS: Then why didn't you go to the office and ask for
12   help?

13   RYAN: Because I couldn't find the office!

14   MRS. MILLS: Mr. Hodges, watch your tone of voice with me!

15   RYAN: I'm sorry.

16   MRS. MILLS: Class, is anyone else having trouble finding their
17   way around school? *(CASSIE raises her hand.)* Yes, Cassie?

18   CASSIE: Well, on the first day of school I accidentally went to
19   lunch during third period instead of fourth.

20   MRS. MILLS: But did you get lost?

21   CASSIE: No, Ma'am.

22   MRS. MILLS: And have you been late to class?

23   CASSIE: No, Ma'am.

24   MRS. MILLS: And do you think you could find the Z-14 hall?

25   CASSIE: Yes, Ma'am, because I have a class in the Z-15 hall, so
26   I'd be just one hall over.

27   MRS. MILLS: Then could you please come up here and explain
28   to Mr. Hodges how to find the Z-14 hall?

29   CASSIE: Sure. *(Goes to the front of the classroom. Takes RYAN'S*
30   *map.)* OK, here's the front of the school.

31   RYAN: But I'm not coming from the front of the school!

32   MRS. MILLS: Do you always have to make everything so
33   difficult?

34   CASSIE: It's OK. So where do you start?

35   RYAN: *(Takes out his schedule.)* OK, from Hall G-22 I go to Hall Z-14.

1   CASSIE: OK, that's easy. Look.

2   MRS. MILLS: Are you paying attention, Mr. Hodges?

3   RYAN: Yes, Ma'am.

4   CASSIE: So here you are at Hall G-22, right?

5   RYAN: Right.

6   CASSIE: *(Points to the map.)* So you take a right here, then two

7   quick lefts, then another right, up the stairs to the S-Wing,

8   another right, up one more flight of stairs to the W-Hall,

9   an immediate left, a little curve to the right and a quick

10   left and there you are! Hall Z-14!

11   RYAN: A right, then two quick lefts, then what?

12   CASSIE: Do you want me to use my highlighter on your map?

13   MRS. MILLS: Oh my gosh! You'd think this was rocket science!

14   Mr. Hodges, was Cassie not clear enough on the

15   directions?

16   RYAN: Sure, but ... OK, it's a right, a left, another left, up the

17   stairs, then right or left ... *(Screams in frustration)* I can't

18   remember! How am I supposed to remember all that?

19   CASSIE: *(Trying to be helpful)* Mrs. Mills, I can highlight this for

20   Ryan.

21   MRS. MILLS: Class, does anyone else have trouble

22   understanding these directions? *(Pause)* Anyone? Janie, do

23   you think you could find your way to Hall Z-14?

24   JANIE: Yes, Ma'am.

25   MRS. MILLS: Could you come up here and give Ryan the

26   directions one more time since he's never even been to his

27   class in Hall Z-14?

28   JANIE: *(Moves to the front of the class.)* Yes, Ma'am. *(Takes the*

29   *map.)* You're starting from Hall G-22, right?

30   RYAN: Mrs. Mills, is this really necessary? I'll study my map

31   tonight, OK?

32   MRS. MILLS: But you need to find your math class in Hall Z-14

33   today, isn't that correct, Mr. Hodges?

34   RYAN: Yes, but ...

35   MRS. MILLS: Go ahead, Janie.

1 JANIE: *(Holding up map)* **OK, starting from Hall G-22, you take**
2   **a right, then a left, then another left, then a right, go up**
3   **the stairs to the S-Wing, then take a right, then up another**
4   **flight of stairs to the W-Hall, then a left, then turn right**
5   **here, turn quickly to the right and there you are. Got it?**
6 RYAN: **No! No, I don't have it!**
7 MRS. MILLS: *(Shaking head, frustrated)* **Mr. Hodges, do you have**
8   **any sense of direction?**
9 RYAN: **Sense of direction, yes, but finding my way around a**
10   **hundred different halls, no!**
11 JANIE: **Maybe I should write it down for him.**
12 RYAN: **Do you mind?**
13 MRS. MILLS: **And what's going to happen when you enter the**
14   **real world, Mr. Hodges? When you learn to drive and have**
15   **to find your way around the city? Are you going to drive**
16   **around all day and miss work because you couldn't find**
17   **the correct street?**
18 RYAN: **No, I'll probably have a GPS. Hey, maybe I need a GPS for**
19   **school!** *(He laughs, but the others don't.)*
20 MRS. MILLS: **That wasn't funny.**
21 RYAN: **Obviously not.**
22 JANIE: **I have a suggestion.**
23 MRS. MILLS: **Yes, Janie?**
24 JANIE: **I could stay after school and teach him how to find his**
25   **way around.**
26 CASSIE: **I could help, too.**
27 MRS. MILLS: **Thank you, girls. That's very nice of you.**
28 RYAN: **I'm not staying after school!**
29 MRS. MILLS: **I don't see that you have a choice, Mr. Hodges.**
30 RYAN: *(Halfway laughing)* **I don't need two girls showing me**
31   **how to get to my classes.**
32 MRS. MILLS: **Mr. Hodges, how many days have you been in this**
33   **school?**
34 RYAN: **Three.**
35 MRS. MILLS: **And how many times have you been late for my**

1   class?

2 RYAN: Three.

3 MRS. MILLS: And how many classes have you been late for, not

4   including mine?

5 RYAN: Not counting the classes I never went to because I

6   couldn't find them?

7 MRS. MILLS: Yes!

8 RYAN: All of them. I've either been late or never went because

9   I was lost.

10 MRS. MILLS: And you don't need help after school learning

11   your way around?

12 RYAN: I don't think so.

13 MRS. MILLS: Quick! How do you get to Hall Z-14?

14 RYAN: Uh, a right, a left, uh, another right, uh, up the stairs ...

15 MRS. MILLS: Wrong! Cassie, Janie, plan on helping Mr. Hodges

16   after school.

17 RYAN: But ...

18 MRS. MILLS: And plan to go over it again and again if that's

19   what it takes!

20 RYAN: But ...

21 MRS. MILLS: Thank you, girls. And Mr. Hodges, tomorrow ...

22   don't be late!

23 RYAN: But ...

24 JANIE: And remember, Ryan, each flight of stairs has its own

25   letter, too. A-F stairs are on the first floor.

26 CASSIE: G-L stairs are on the second floor.

27 JANIE: M and N are a little confusing because they go down to

28   the basement, but if you accidentally go down there and

29   get lost, just take the B-1 or B-14 hall back to the main

30   stairs, then you can start from the beginning.

31 CASSIE: And you can always go to the office.

32 RYAN: Wherever that is.

33 CASSIE: It's behind the band hall. See, you come in through the

34   main entrance, take a right at the teacher's lounge, quick

35   left at the cafeteria, turn down the D hall, take the E stairs

1   to the second floor, then another right to the G stairs, but

2   remember, don't take the M stairs because that'll take you

3   back down to the basement, and then ...

4 RYAN: Whoa! Wait! Stop! Please, stop!

5 MRS. MILLS: Confused again, Mr. Hodges?

6 RYAN: Confused? Yes, I'm confused! Confused out of my mind!

7 MRS. MILLS: *(Shaking her head)* Some students just try my

8   patience.

9 JANIE: It's not that hard, Ryan.

10 CASSIE: Really!

11 MRS. MILLS: All right, everyone back in their seats. Why don't

12   we spend the rest of the class time doing something else

13   besides teaching Mr. Hodges how to find his way around

14   the school! All right, everyone open their books to chapter

15   two. Mr. Hodges, do you need help finding chapter two?

3. A Change of Attitude

CAST: (2M, 1F) JAVIER, DEREK, TRINA
PROPS: Lunch trays, utensils, glass of water.

1   *(At rise JAVIER and DEREK are sitting at a table in a*
2   *lunchroom.)*
3   **JAVIER:** *(Eating, with his mouth full)* **Derek, what's wrong with**
4   **you? Why aren't you eating?**
5   **DEREK: Because I'm fat!**
6   **JAVIER: What?**
7   **DEREK: I'm fat!**
8   **JAVIER: That's ridiculous! You're not fat!**
9   **DEREK: Yes, I am!** *(Stands, squeezes his stomach.)* **See?**
10   **JAVIER: No.**
11   **DEREK:** *(Continues to squeeze his stomach.)* **Look! See?**
12   **JAVIER: Quit being stupid. Sit down and eat. You're not fat.**
13   **DEREK:** *(Sits down.)* **Do you know how many calories are in a**
14   **kernel of corn?**
15   **JAVIER: I don't know? Maybe one?**
16   **DEREK: Then I'll only eat like fifty or something. That should**
17   **get me through the day.** *(Eats a kernel.)* **One. Two.**
18   *(Continues to eat and count.)*
19   **TRINA:** *(Enters carrying a lunch tray.)* **Hey, guys.**
20   **JAVIER: Hey, Trina.**
21   **DEREK: Three ... four ... five ...**
22   **TRINA: Derek, why are you counting kernels of corn?**
23   **DEREK: I'm counting calories.**
24   **TRINA: Why?**
25   **JAVIER: He's on a diet.**

1　TRINA: Why?

2　DEREK: Six ... seven ... eight ...

3　JAVIER: He thinks he's fat.

4　TRINA: Derek, you're not fat!

5　JAVIER: Stupid, huh?

6　DEREK: Nine ... I know I'm stupid.

7　JAVIER: Then quit counting kernels of corn!

8　DEREK: Ten ... eleven ... Yeah, I'm stupid. I can never do

9　　　　anything right.

10　JAVIER: That's not true. You passed that pop quiz in geography

11　　　　this morning. So obviously you did something right.

12　DEREK: It was luck.

13　TRINA: Derek, what's really bothering you?

14　DEREK: Besides hating myself? Nothing.

15　JAVIER: You hate yourself?

16　TRINA: Derek, you don't hate yourself!

17　DEREK: Twelve ... thirteen ... Yes, I do. Fourteen, fifteen ...

18　JAVIER: Hey, I don't hate you.

19　DEREK: You did yesterday.

20　TRINA: What happened yesterday?

21　JAVIER: That's because you caused me to get into trouble!

22　TRINA: How? What happened?

23　DEREK: Don't ask.

24　JAVIER: Actually, it was funny. Except for the part of me getting

25　　　　thrown out of history class.

26　TRINA: What happened? Tell me!

27　JAVIER: OK, so, Derek, Mr. Funny Guy here, stuffed chalk

28　　　　under his gums and acted like a walrus! And I couldn't

29　　　　stop laughing. I mean seriously, I couldn't stop! Mr.

30　　　　Rodriguez was like, "Javier, for the last time, I'm warning

31　　　　you ... !"

32　DEREK: Sorry I made you laugh, Javier.

33　JAVIER: No, that was funny! But what made me mad was that I

34　　　　was thrown out of class! Which means I get Saturday

35　　　　detention! Yeah, I was mad yesterday, but forget it, I'm

1   over it now.

2   DEREK: I'm sorry! I'm stupid, OK? Now, where was I? Sixteen ...

3   seventeen ... eighteen. Stupid and fat!

4   TRINA: Derek, why are you always so down on yourself?

5   DEREK: I guess because every morning when I get out of bed, I

6   look in the mirror and face the agonizing truth.

7   JAVIER: What? You got another zit?

8   DEREK: That I'm ugly!

9   TRINA: You aren't ugly! Is he, Javier?

10 JAVIER: Don't ask me! I mean, hey, I don't look at other guys

11   like that! 'Cause when I look at you Derek, I don't think,

12   "Gosh, that's one ugly dude!" Or, "Dang, that's one good-

13   looking guy!" Sorry, but that's just not the way I am. But I

14   can tell you this, Derek, you're not fat!

15 TRINA: And you're not ugly!

16 DEREK: You're just trying to be nice to me. Because ... you feel

17   sorry for me.

18 JAVIER: Why would I feel sorry for you? You're the one who

19   passed the pop quiz in geography class today. Not me. So

20   feel sorry for me, OK?

21 TRINA: Derek, you need to be more positive.

22 DEREK: I'm positive that I'm a loser!

23 TRINA: Why are you trying so hard to convince yourself that

24   you're a loser?

25 JAVIER: And fat! And ugly!

26 TRINA: Javier!

27 DEREK: I think I'm going to cut out all carbs.

28 JAVIER: Uh ... Those corn kernels that you're eating are all

29   carbs.

30 DEREK: They are? I thought they were a vegetable.

31 JAVIER: Starch city!

32 DEREK: Well, no more carbs, sugar, or red meat!

33 TRINA: What's wrong with red meat?

34 DEREK: I don't know, but I read in *The Enquirer* that a lot of

35   movie stars don't eat carbs, sugar, or red meat. So there

1   must be something to it. In fact, I think I'll cut out all
2   calories. Maybe I'll go on a water diet.
3 JAVIER: A water diet?
4 DEREK: Nothing but water!
5 JAVIER: What? Till you blow away? *(Waves.)* Bye, Derek! It was
6   nice knowing you.
7 DEREK: Well, that would probably be a good thing. Me blowing
8   away. Maybe I'll just blow away to another continent. Say,
9   Hawaii ...
10 TRINA: Uh, Derek ... Hawaii is not a continent. It's a state.
11 JAVIER: An island.
12 TRINA: A state.
13 JAVIER: Actually, a group of islands.
14 TRINA: Well, it's both ... but it's not a continent. Now if you blew
15   away to Europe or Africa or Australia ...
16 JAVIER: That's funny that you thought Hawaii was a continent!
17   And you passed the geography pop quiz! Did you cheat?
18 DEREK: No! I told you, it was luck! So see, I am dumb!
19 JAVIER: If you think Hawaii's a continent ...
20 DEREK: I forgot, OK! Forget it! I am stupid! And ugly and fat!
21   Now, where was I? Do you know where I was? Oh yeah, I'm
22   not eating carbs. *(Pushes tray away.)* I'm drinking water.
23   *(Takes a long drink.)*
24 TRINA: I think your problem is something else, Derek.
25 JAVIER: Trina, don't help Derek find any more negative
26   features in himself.
27 DEREK: It's OK, Trina. I know I don't have any likable
28   qualities. I'm stupid. I'm fat. I'm ugly. I'm too short. My
29   teeth are crooked. I have no sense of style. My eyes are the
30   wrong color. My shoes are probably the wrong color. I hate
31   my hair. And my feet stink.
32 TRINA: Derek, stop it!
33 JAVIER: Your feet stink?
34 DEREK: Yeah. Do you want to see? I mean, smell?
35 JAVIER: Uh, no. I'll pass. But thanks.

1   TRINA: Derek, let me tell you what your real problem is.
2   DEREK: Sure, Trina. Tell me.
3   JAVIER: Trina, are you sure you're helping here?
4   DEREK: It's OK, Trina. Tell me.
5   TRINA: *(Taps his head.)* It's what's going on inside of here.
6   DEREK: I know. I'm dumb.
7   TRINA: Derek, your problem is low self-esteem.
8   DEREK: Thanks, Trina. I'll add that to my list. Low self-esteem.
9   TRINA: Which means you don't like yourself.
10 DEREK: I know.
11 TRINA: But don't you see? It's all your fault!
12 DEREK: I know. Everything is always my fault.
13 JAVIER: Trina, is this supposed to be helping?
14 TRINA: Listen, Derek, you see the worst in yourself because of
15   your negative thoughts.
16 DEREK: I know.
17 JAVIER: Not some light bulb explanation here, Trina.
18 TRINA: Which means ... you need to take stock of your inner
19   talk.
20 DEREK: Huh?
21 TRINA: Change the way you talk to yourself.
22 DEREK: How?
23 JAVIER: I know! *(Jumps up.)* I'm not fat! I'm hot!
24 DEREK: *(Gives JAVIER a strange look.)* Like that?
25 TRINA: Well, kinda ...
26 JAVIER: *(Sits down.)* You try it, Derek.
27 TRINA: Yeah, go ahead. Try it, Derek.
28 DEREK: *(Stands. Dryly)* I'm not fat. I'm hot.
29 TRINA: *(Trying to be enthusiastic)* Well, that was a good try!
30   Because see, when you say positive things about yourself,
31   then you start to feel positive about yourself. See?
32 DEREK: I guess.
33 TRINA: Besides, we can do little to change the way we look, but
34   we can change our attitude. And with the right attitude,
35   you feel good about yourself!

1   JAVIER: *(Jumps up.)* I love myself!

2   TRINA: *(Gives JAVIER a strange look.)* So instead of saying, "I'm

3   stupid" say, "I'm smart!"

4   JAVIER: I'm smart! *(Short pause)* Even though I flunked the

5   geography quiz. But I tried! Even though I didn't study.

6   But I meant to! And next time I'll pass it! *(Sits down.)*

7   TRINA: See? That's the attitude!

8   DEREK: But even with all that positive inner talk, I still have a

9   problem.

10   TRINA: What's that?

11   DEREK: No one likes me.

12   TRINA: That's not true!

13   JAVIER: *(Jumps up.)* Everyone loves me! And if you don't, well,

14   you should!

15   TRINA: *(Gives JAVIER a strange look.)* Derek, you've got to stop

16   with all the negative talk. When you catch yourself saying

17   something like, "No one likes me," stop and say something

18   positive. Like, "Trina likes me. Javier likes me." And

19   remember, there are more important qualities than just

20   looks.

21   DEREK: Like what?

22   TRINA: Like how you treat others. Most people will like you

23   because of how you treat them.

24   JAVIER: I love you, man!

25   TRINA: Because when you treat others with kindness and

26   respect – even when they don't deserve it ...

27   JAVIER: I don't deserve it, man!

28   TRINA: Then you can feel good about yourself. Because it's not

29   how you look, but how you relate to others.

30   DEREK: Thanks, Trina. I think I get it. Treat others with

31   kindness and respect and change the way I talk to myself.

32   TRINA: Exactly!

33   JAVIER: That's right! It's all in the attitude! Like this! *(Stands,*

34   *halfway singing and dancing.)* Because I'm good, I'm good

35   ... yeah, yeah, I'm good!

1   DEREK: Well, I am the one who passed the geography quiz. So
2   that means I'm smart. And I'm not that bad looking. And
3   you know what else?
4   TRINA: What?
5   DEREK: I'm hungry! Forget that water diet! I'm eating!
6   JAVIER: *(Still standing)* Because I'm good, I'm good ... yeah,
7   yeah, I'm good ... Heck, I'm great!
8   TRINA: Javier, I think that's enough.
9   JAVIER: I'm just trying to help.
10   DEREK: *(His mouth full)* It's OK, Javier. I got it.
11   JAVIER: But I just want to tell the world! Because I'm good, I'm
12   good ... yeah, yeah, I'm good! *(He continues.)* I'm good, I'm
13   good ... yeah, yeah, I'm good ...
14   TRINA: And see, Derek, the opposite of having a low self-
15   esteem is having too much self-esteem. *(Points to JAVIER.*
16   *DEREK nods as they watch JAVIER who continues.)* And that
17   will drive people away!

4. Love Is All You Need

CAST: (2M, 3F) BAILEY, TOM, AMBER, JED, MONICA

1   *(At rise the characters are lined up across the stage in the*
2   *order in which they speak. They stare straight ahead.)*
3   **BAILEY:** *(Looks over at TOM.)* **Tom is the most amazing guy.**
4   **He's cute, smart, funny ... Yesterday during math class, he**
5   **did this hilarious impression of Mr. Bates. I laughed so**
6   **hard, I cried. I wish he would notice me.**
7   **TOM:** *(Looks over at AMBER.)* **Amber doesn't know this, but my**
8   **heart is totally wrapped around her little finger. One little**
9   **smile from her and it's ...** *(Thumps on chest with hand)* **Ba-**
10   **boom, ba-boom, ba-boom. I wish she would notice me.**
11   **AMBER:** *(Looks over at JED.)* **Jed doesn't even know that I'm**
12   **alive. I know that's a stupid saying, but it's true. But that**
13   **doesn't mean I can't dream, does it?** *(Smiling)* **There we**
14   **are, hand in hand, running through a field of wildflowers.**
15   **He looks at me ... I look at him ... and then ... and then ...**
16   **Well ... I wish he would notice me.**
17   **JED:** *(Looks over at MONICA.)* **Monica must think I'm a dork. I**
18   **smile, nothing. I pass her a note, she rolls her eyes. I**
19   **accidentally run into her on purpose, she yells at me.**
20   **What's the problem? What's wrong with me? Hey, I'm a**
21   **great guy! I wish she would notice me.**
22   **MONICA:** *(Looks heavenward, then smiles.)* **J.D. Samuels. Yes, *the***
23   **J.D. Samuels is the finest actor in the entire world! I bet he's**
24   **nominated for an Oscar this year. Oh, if only my dad would**
25   **get transferred to Hollywood! Then I could leave this dull**
26   **town and find a way to cross paths with him. And then, I'm**

1   sure he'd notice me! It'd probably be love at first sight!

2   BAILEY: *(Steps out, circles TOM, then stands in front of him.)*

3   He's the one. I know he is. And we would make a perfect

4   couple. I can see it now. He finally notices me, *(Glances*

5   *back at him)* sees my adoring face, and little hearts begin

6   the flicker in his eyes. Yes, it's definitely love.

7   TOM: *(Steps out from behind BAILEY and stands in front of*

8   *AMBER.)* If only Amber would give me a chance. Then

9   she'd see what she's been missing. I'd tell jokes and she'd

10   laugh. We would be like ... like my favorite sitcom on TV!

11   Finishing each other's lines, throwing punch lines, quick

12   comebacks ... it'd be great!

13   AMBER: *(Steps out from behind TOM, circles JED, then stands in*

14   *front of him.)* We sit on a blanket in the soft grass,

15   surrounded by flowers, as he reads love sonnets to me.

16   "How do I love thee, let me count the ways ... " The sun is

17   warm and comforting, the breeze light, and then ... and

18   then he reaches out to touch my face ... *(She smiles.)*

19   JED: *(Rushes out from behind AMBER, then stands in front of*

20   *MONICA.)* I need to get her attention! Not more attention

21   that causes her to roll her eyes, but the attention that

22   causes her to fall at my feet! Wait, not fall at my feet. Melt.

23   Yes, I want to make her heart melt!

24   MONICA: *(Steps out from behind JED.)* J.D. Samuels would make

25   any girl's heart melt. I would just die to meet him! I know!

26   Maybe I should send him a letter. Not a fan letter, but a

27   letter expressing my love for him. Yeah! And I'll include

28   my newest school picture. I hope he thinks I'm cute!

29   JED: *(Stands in front of MONICA.)* I need to get Monica's

30   attention! Skywriting! Yes! *(Moves his hand above him to*

31   *illustrate.)* Jed loves Monica! Yeah! No ... I couldn't afford

32   that. Let's see ... I know! A poster hung in every hallway at

33   school. Jed loves Monica! I wonder if she'd think it was

34   romantic? Maybe. Red. The posters should be red. *(He*

35   *nods.)*

1   AMBER: *(Steps in front of JED.)* I'll admit it, I'm a romantic at
2   heart. Little love notes, poems, flowers, walking in the
3   rain ... Isn't that what love is supposed to be about?
4   Holding hands. Laughing. Looking into each other's eyes.
5   Maybe I should do something romantic so Jed will notice
6   me. Cookies! I could bake him cookies!
7   TOM: *(Steps in front of AMBER.)* Here's one for you! Knock,
8   knock! *(Imitates a girl's voice.)* Who's there? *(His voice.)*
9   Adore. *(Girl voice.)* Adore who? *(His voice.)* Adore stands
10   betweens us! *(Laughs.)* I wonder if Amber likes jokes? I'm
11   not really the romantic type, but if she wants to laugh ...
12   I'm the guy for her!
13 BAILEY: *(Steps in front of TOM.)* He's the funniest guy I've ever met!
14   I love his jokes! Especially his knock-knock jokes! He always
15   keeps the classes at school laughing. Especially me. I guess
16   you could say he's a class clown, but that's just the kind of guy
17   I'm looking for. *(ALL return to their original places.)*
18 TOM: *(Turns to AMBER.)* Hey, you want to hear a knock-knock joke?
19 AMBER: No, thanks.
20 TOM: You don't?
21 AMBER: No. I don't like jokes. But thanks anyway.
22 TOM: *(Disappointed.)* You don't like jokes?
23 AMBER: No.
24 BAILEY: I do!
25 TOM: You do?
26 BAILEY: I love jokes!
27 TOM: Really?
28 BAILEY: Uh-huh.
29 TOM: You want to hear a knock-knock joke?
30 BAILEY: You bet!
31 TOM: Knock, knock.
32 BAILEY: Who's there?
33 TOM: Watson.
34 BAILEY: Watson who?
35 TIM: Watson TV tonight?

1 **BAILEY:** *(Laughs.)* **I love that! You are so funny!**

2 **TOM: Really?**

3 **BAILEY: Really!** *(TOM and BAILEY exit.)*

4 **JED:** *(Turns to MONICA.)* **Love makes the world go around.**

5 **MONICA: What?**

6 **JED: Love makes heavy things light.**

7 **MONICA: What are you talking about?**

8 **JED: Love has no errors.**

9 **MONICA: What?**

10 **JED: Love is the flower of life.**

11 **MONICA: I don't know what you're talking about.**

12 **JED: Love is not bought.**

13 **MONICA: You make no sense to me.**

14 **JED: Love is all you need.**

15 **MONICA: Yes, love. I love J.D. Samuels.**

16 **JED: Who is J.D. Samuels?**

17 **MONICA:** *(Shocked he doesn't know him)* **Who is J.D. Samuels?**

18 **Who is J.D. Samuels?**

19 **JED: Yeah, who is J.D. Samuels?**

20 **MONICA: The movie star! You know! J.D. Samuels!**

21 **JED: Guess I don't know him.**

22 **MONICA: And I'm in love with him!**

23 **JED: You are?**

24 **MONICA: Yes! And I need to go write him a letter.** *(Starts off.)* **I**

25 **wonder if he'll write me back? Maybe I should include my**

26 **phone number. I wonder if he could get me a part in his**

27 **next movie? Maybe I could be his next leading lady.** *(JED*

28 *and AMBER stand side by side for a moment.)*

29 **AMBER: Love is not a choice, but is fate.**

30 **JED: What?**

31 **AMBER: "How do I love thee. Let me count the ways."**

32 **JED: That's nice.**

33 **AMBER: I'm a romantic at heart.**

34 **JED: Me, too!** *(Pause as they look at each other, reach out and take*

35 *hands, and exit.)*

5. Dear Diary

CAST: (2M, 2F) TAYLOR, DAD, MEGAN, MOM
PROPS: Diary, pen, plate of cookies, milk, cell phone.
SETTING: Taylor's bedroom.

1   *(At rise TAYLOR is sitting in his room writing in a diary.)*
2   **TAYLOR:** *(Writes.)* **Dear Diary, Today was the worst day of my**
3   **life. My dad found out about my little experiment.**
4   **Needless to say, dad was not impressed with my idea of**
5   **attaching fan blades to the dog's tail with Super glue.**
6   **DAD:** *(From the side of the stage)* **What were you thinking,**
7   **Taylor?**
8   **TAYLOR:** *(Writes.)* **I thought it was a good idea. Tail wags back**
9   **and forth, then, ahhhh ... fresh air.**
10 **DAD: And you expect our dog to run around the house with fan**
11   **blades attached to his tail?**
12 **TAYLOR:** *(Writes.)* **And, oddly enough, Jasper didn't seem to**
13   **mind.**
14 **DAD: I want you to take them off now! And I mean** *now!*
15 **TAYLOR:** *(Writes.)* **Everyone, except for me, knows that Super**
16   **glue doesn't come out easily. So, unfortunately, our little**
17   **poodle's tail looks deformed now. Poor Jasper.**
18 **DAD: Taylor, for the rest of the day, don't plan on going**
19   **anywhere! And there'll be no TV and no video games! It'll**
20   **be chores and homework tonight, got it?** *(Exits.)*
21 **TAYLOR:** *(Writes.)* **So, if that wasn't bad enough ... Well, maybe**
22   **I should explain first. Mom, being mom, felt sorry for me**
23   **because I'd spent two hours cutting fan blades out of**
24   **Jasper's tail and then went straight to my room to do**
25   **homework. Well, I was about to start homework, but I**
26   **wanted to check my e-mail first. No crime in that, right?**

1   **MOM:** *(Enters on the side of the stage. Smiling, she holds a plate*
2   *of cookies and a glass of milk.)* **Doing your homework,**
3   **Sweetheart?**
4   **TAYLOR:** *(Writes.)* **When all of a sudden, Mom barges into my**
5   **room! "Just checking my e-mail, Mom."**
6   **MOM:** *(Screams, dropping cookies.)* ***Taylor Don Jenkins!***
7   **TAYLOR: What? Whoa! Where did that come from! Mom, I**
8   **didn't ... ! It just popped up! I don't know how it got there!"**
9   **MOM:** *What do you think you're doing?*
10   **TAYLOR: I didn't do that! I mean, it just appeared out of**
11   **nowhere!**
12   **MOM: How could you?**
13   **TAYLOR: I ... I ...**
14   **MOM: I'm so disappointed in you!**
15   **TAYLOR: But ... I ...**
16   **MOM: That's it, Taylor! You get off the computer right this very**
17   **second! And stay off!** *(Exits.)*
18   **TAYLOR:** *(Writes.)* **So, now we're getting Internet protection.**
19   **Yeah, that's right. And until then ... well, diary, it's just you**
20   **and me.** *(Short pause as he taps his pen.)* **Oh, but this was**
21   **not the end of my wonderful day. Megan, my girlfriend,**
22   **called out of the blue and started screaming at me.**
23   **MEGAN:** *(Enters on the side of the stage, talking into the phone.)*
24   **How could you not notice, Taylor? Are you blind?**
25   **TAYLOR: Notice? Notice what?**
26   **MEGAN: Notice what?**
27   **TAYLOR:** *(Writing.)* **So, I'm panicking here. What am I**
28   **supposed to notice?**
29   **MEGAN: I'm not telling you!**
30   **TAYLOR: I don't see it. I'm trying, but I don't.**
31   **MEGAN: And don't you dare guess!**
32   **TAYLOR: Don't guess? Make something up? Hurry! Quick!**
33   **Think!**
34   **MEGAN: Tell me! What is different about me today? And you**
35   **better get this right!**

1 TAYLOR: I better get this right? And if I don't?

2 MEGAN: 'Cause if you can't even notice a major change like

3   this, Taylor, then obviously you don't really care about me!

4 TAYLOR: I noticed! I noticed! *(Writes.)* I'm lying through my

5   teeth.

6 MEGAN: Then tell me!

7 TAYLOR: Quick! Think!

8 MEGAN: Tell me!

9 TAYLOR: Your eyes ...

10 MEGAN: My eyes?

11 TAYLOR: Are bluer than the day before. *(Writes.)* I thought it

12   sounded good. Romantic.

13 MEGAN: Wrong! So you didn't notice, did you? And you don't

14   really love me, do you?

15 TAYLOR: I do, it's just ...

16 MEGAN: It's over, Taylor! You and me ... we're over!

17 TAYLOR: Over? Wait! What did I miss here? What did I not

18   notice?

19 MEGAN: You just look right past me, don't you? A major change

20   and you don't even notice! Thanks, Taylor! Thanks a lot!

21 TAYLOR: No, no, I noticed!

22 MEGAN: You're lying!

23 TAYLOR: No! You ... you look so beautiful every day! *(Writes.)*

24   You'd think that line would get me somewhere, wouldn't

25   you? But no ...

26 MEGAN: Oh, nice try, Taylor! Like I said, just forget it! It's over!

27 TAYLOR: It's over?

28 MEGAN: I'm breaking up!

29 TAYLOR: Over something I didn't notice?

30 MEGAN: That and everything else!

31 TAYLOR: Everything else? What's everything else? *(Writing.)*

32   Girls are so hard to understand.

33 MEGAN: You ... you just don't understand. And I can't believe I

34   spent three months with you and now it's this ... *(Begins to*

35   *cry.)*

1   TAYLOR: And now comes the guilt. She's crying. Probably fake
2   tears, but it's working.
3   MEGAN: *(Crying.)* I'm really hurt, Taylor.
4   TAYLOR: I'm really confused, Megan.
5   MEGAN: OK, I'll tell you.
6   TAYLOR: Finally!
7   MEGAN: I cut my hair, you idiot!
8   TAYLOR: You did?
9   MEGAN: Yes I did and you didn't notice!
10   TAYLOR: I'm sorry, Megan! Like I said, you always look
11   beautiful to me. So, how much did you cut off?
12   MEGAN: *(Crying.)* Two inches!
13   TAYLOR: And I was supposed to notice?
14   MEGAN: Yes!
15   TAYLOR: Oh my gosh! *(Stands, leaves diary, moves to the*
16   *opposite end of the stage and talks into a phone.)* Oh my
17   gosh! You want to break up with me for not noticing that
18   you cut two inches off your hair?
19   MEGAN: *(Sniffling)* Yes. *(MOM and DAD enter behind TAYLOR.)*
20   TAYLOR: Megan, you are so stupid! And obviously you have no
21   brains, either! Maybe you need to Super glue some
22   common sense into your head so you can figure out when
23   you make no sense whatsoever!
24   DAD: Son, that's enough!
25   MOM: Taylor!
26   TAYLOR: *(Into the phone)* I have to go.
27   DAD: Taylor, you are to never speak to anyone like that!
28   Especially a young woman!
29   MOM: What were you thinking, Taylor? Did I not teach you any
30   manners?
31   TAYLOR: But ...
32   DAD: *(Holds out hand.)* Hand it over. No cell phone. No TV. No
33   video games.
34   MOM: And no computer!
35   DAD: For a week!

1 **TAYLOR: A week?**

2 **MOM: And I want you to give the dog a bath. Poor thing.** *(MOM*

3 *and DAD exit.)*

4 **TAYLOR:** *(Returns to the diary. Writes.)* **I guess this is what life**

5 **was like in the olden days. Before computers, cell phones**

6 **and video games. And it sucks. Well, I'll write more later. I**

7 **have to go bathe the dog.** *(Stands, as he is leaving.)* **I still**

8 **thought it was a good idea. Jasper wags his tail ... then**

9 **ahhhh ... fresh air.**

6. Star Search

CAST: (3F) MABLE, ROCHELLE, KELLIE
PROPS: Tissues.

1 MABLE: We need to decide on a talent act for the competition.

2 ROCHELLE: One that we can perform together.

3 KELLIE: *(As if twirling batons)* How about fire batons?

4 ROCHELLE: Kellie, we don't know how to twirl! Do you want us
5   to catch our hair on fire?

6 KELLIE: We could learn.

7 MABLE: In one week?

8 KELLIE: It was just an idea.

9 ROCHELLE: Sing?

10 KELLIE: Great idea.

11 MABLE: Except I can't sing. Guys, you know that.

12 ROCHELLE: That's true. When you sing along with the radio ...
13   well, it's painful.

14 KELLIE: Well, Rochelle and I could sing and you could just
15   mouth the words.

16 MABLE: No! I want to be a part of this talent competition and
17   not just stand there like this. *(Mimes moving her mouth.)*

18 ROCHELLE: Mable is right. Let's think of something else.

19 KELLIE: A magic show?

20 ROCHELLE: With three people?

21 KELLIE: Well, you could be the magician and Mable could be
22   the attendant and you could make me disappear.

23 MABLE: I wish.

24 ROCHELLE: There are already a couple of people doing magic
25   shows. We need something different.

26 KELLIE: How about if we make up a dance to a cool song?

1   MABLE: And what if we get stuck performing after the
2   Mendoza sisters?

3   ROCHELLE: Oh, that would be bad. We'd look like idiots.

4   MABLE: Those girls can dance!

5   ROCHELLE: So, we need to think of something else.

6   KELLIE: How about if we perform a dramatic scene?

7   MABLE: That's actually not a bad idea. And we could also write
8   our own script.

9   ROCHELLE: I like that idea.

10 KELLIE: Yeah, and we could perform something so dramatic
11   it'd bring the audience to tears.

12 MABLE: That'd definitely get us first place in this year's Star
13   Search.

14 KELLIE: So let's play around with some ideas.

15 MABLE: Something intense.

16 ROCHELLE: Emotionally grabbing.

17 KELLIE: Tear-jerking. *(After a short pause she puts her hand to*
18   *her head, dramatically.)* **The pain! The misery! How can I**
19   **go on?**

20 MABLE: *(Rolling her eyes)* **We don't know.**

21 KELLIE: *(Dramatically)* **He sliced my heart into a million pieces!**

22 ROCHELLE: This is a three-person show, Kellie! Remember?

23 KELLIE: And all I want to do is die! There is no life for me now!
24   I can't go on!

25 MABLE: So what are Rochelle and I supposed to do? Stand
26   around and comfort you?

27 KELLIE: The pain! Oh, the pain! All I want to do is die! *(Looks*
28   *heavenward.)* **Please, just let me die!**

29 ROCHELLE: *(Grabs MABLE'S arm. In a dramatic tone)* **How can**
30   **we watch this?**

31 MABLE: It's painful! Oh, so painful!

32 KELLIE: *(Falls to her knees.)* **Why did he do this to me? Why?**

33 ROCHELLE: *(To MABLE)* **Why?**

34 MABLE: *(To ROCHELLE)* **Why?**

35 KELLIE: He proclaimed his love for me, promised me the

1   world, swore he would never, ever leave me ... *(Falls to the*
2   *ground)* **Then he left me! Oh, oh, oh!**
3 **ROCHELLE:** *(Trying not to laugh)* **I need a tissue!**
4 **MABLE: Me too!** *(They find a tissue to wipe their fake tears.)* **How**
5   **can we watch our dearest friend in such agony?**
6 **ROCHELLE: What shall we do?**
7 **KELLIE: Oh! Oh, the pain! Oh, my heart!**
8 **MABLE: Well, you know what they say.**
9 **ROCHELLE: No, what do they say?**
10 **MABLE: This, too, shall pass.**
11 **ROCHELLE: But when?**
12 **MABLE: Hopefully very soon.**
13 **KELLIE:** *(Looks up. In a normal voice)* **Say it's killing you to**
14   **watch me die!**
15 **MABLE: You're dying?**
16 **KELLIE: Yes!**
17 **ROCHELLE:** *(Dramatically, trying not to laugh)* **Mable, I think**
18   **she's dying!**
19 **MABLE: No! You can't be serious!**
20 **KELLIE: Oh, I'm dying! Dying! Dying!**
21 **ROCHELLE: Kellie, listen to me.**
22 **KELLIE: I can't! I can't! I must leave this earth if I can't be with**
23   **him!**
24 **MABLE: Help her, Rochelle!**
25 **ROCHELLE: Listen to me, Kellie.**
26 **KELLIE:** *(Looks up.)* **Say you can sympathize with my pain and**
27   **start crying.**
28 **ROCHELLE: Kellie, you have to pull yourself together.**
29 **KELLIE:** *(Looks up.)* **That's not what I said to say!**
30 **MABLE: Rochelle, we have to do something! Look, she's dying!**
31 **ROCHELLE: Well, I wanted to remind her that there are other**
32   **fish in the sea.**
33 **MABLE: That's good advice.**
34 **ROCHELLE: And that if she can't pull herself together she**
35   **should seek professional advice.**

1   **KELLIE:** *(Banging her fist on the floor)* **How could he have done**
2   **this to me? I loved him!**
3   **ROCHELLE: It's quite pathetic, don't you think?**
4   **KELLIE: I loved him! I loved him!**
5   **MABLE: Do you suppose she's unstable?**
6   **ROCHELLE: Apparently so.**
7   **KELLIE: And he took my heart and ripped it out!** *(Falls to the*
8   *ground.)*
9   **MABLE: What should we do?**
10 **KELLIE:** *(Looks up at them.)* **Fall over my body and cry!**
11 **ROCHELLE: I don't know, but we can't just stand here and**
12   **watch.**
13 **MABLE: You're right.** *(ROCHELLE and MABLE look at each other,*
14   *then exit.)*
15 **KELLIE: I'm dying, dying, dying.** *(Looks up.)* **Hey, where did**
16   **ya'll go?**

7. First Kiss

CAST: (1M, 2F) JENNY, BRIANNA, NICK
PROPS: Barbie and Ken dolls. Other Barbie items such as
clothes, accessories, etc., if possible. Lip balm.
SETTING: Yard.

1 *(At rise JENNY and BRIANNA are sitting in the yard with*
2 *Barbie dolls.)*
3 **JENNY:** It's not working.
4 **BRIANNA:** Keep trying.
5 **JENNY:** *(Holding up the Barbie doll)* **Ken, did you just propose?**
6 **BRIANNA:** *(Holding up the Ken doll, talking in a deep voice)* **Yes,**
7 **Barbie. I love you. Please say yes.**
8 **JENNY:** I won't accept your proposal unless you get on one
9 knee.
10 **BRIANNA:** Jenny ... *(Changes back to deep voice)* **I mean, Barbie**
11 **... of course, I'll get down on one knee. Barbie, will you**
12 **marry me?**
13 **JENNY:** No, I don't think so.
14 **BRIANNA:** What?
15 **JENNY:** Sorry, Ken, but I'm too young to be tied down.
16 **BRIANNA:** Jenny, you're supposed to say yes! Then Barbie runs
17 **into Ken's arms and they kiss! Come on!** *(Takes Barbie and*
18 *shows them embracing and kissing.)*
19 **JENNY:** That was fine a few years ago, but it's just not fun
20 anymore.
21 **BRIANNA:** But we used to play Barbies for hours and hours.
22 Remember how much fun it was?
23 **JENNY:** I remember, Brianna. And it was my idea to try this
24 again, but ... it's just not the same.
25 **BRIANNA:** Keep trying, Jenny. OK, tell Ken you've had a change

1   **of heart, run into his arms and they can kiss.**

2   **JENNY:** *(Laughs)* **Remember how long we would make them**

3   **kiss?**

4   **BRIANNA: Forever, it seemed.** *(They put Barbie and Ken together*

5   *for a long kiss.)* **I guess we were playing out our own**

6   **dreams of having that first kiss.**

7   **JENNY: The anticipation.**

8   **BRIANNA: The butterflies in your stomach.**

9   **JENNY:** *(As they put Barbie and Ken together again)* **His lips**

10   **meeting yours.**

11   **BRIANNA: Your heart racing.**

12   **JENNY: Your hands sweating.**

13   **BRIANNA: Hoping you would do it right.**

14   **JENNY: Do it right?**

15   **BRIANNA: You know, hoping you weren't a bad kisser.**

16   **JENNY: How hard can it be? It's just ...** *(Puts Barbie and Ken*

17   *together again)* **Kiss, kiss, kiss.**

18   **BRIANNA: But what if something goes wrong?**

19   **JENNY: Like what?**

20   **BRIANNA: Like your teeth bang into each other.**

21   **JENNY: Oh, that'd be embarrassing!**

22   **BRIANNA: Or you're so nervous that your lips are quivering.**

23   **JENNY: Or at that exact moment, you feel a sneeze coming on.**

24   **BRIANNA: Or you choke on your gum.**

25   **JENNY: Or you both lean forward and your noses hit.**

26   **BRIANNA: Ouch.**

27   **JENNY: And you turn your head to the right, but so does he.**

28   **Then you turn your head to the left ...**

29   **BRIANNA: And so does he!**

30   **JENNY: And it's this ...** *(Mimics with Barbie and Ken)* **And that**

31   **first kiss, which was supposed to be the highlight of your**

32   **life, becomes a disaster.**

33   **BRIANNA: An embarrassing disaster.**

34   **JENNY: Yeah, well ... I'm glad that hasn't happened to me.**

35   **BRIANNA: Me too.**

1 JENNY: Of course ...
2 BRIANNA: It couldn't have happened if you've never ... you
3   know.
4 JENNY: What?
5 BRIANNA: Had your first kiss.
6 JENNY: That's true.
7 BRIANNA: So, have you?
8 JENNY: Have you?
9 BRIANNA: I asked you first.
10 JENNY: *(After a pause)* No. *(Quickly)* But I've practiced.
11 BRIANNA: On who?
12 JENNY: You mean, on what.
13 BRIANNA: What?
14 JENNY: My mirror.
15 BRIANNA: Oh! Yeah, I've done that, too.
16 JENNY: So, you've never ... ?
17 BRIANNA: No. And that thing about clunking your teeth
18   together or turning your head the same way really makes
19   me nervous.
20 JENNY: Me too!
21 BRIANNA: *(Holds up Ken.)* Barbie, may I have a kiss?
22 JENNY: *(Holds up Barbie.)* Of course. *(They struggle for several*
23   *minutes, turning their heads the same way, until finally they*
24   *meet for a kiss.)* That was awkward.
25 BRIANNA: And that's what I'm afraid of. Because if someone
26   like Jake Daniels ever wants to kiss me ...
27 JENNY: I bet he's an expert at kissing.
28 BRIANNA: Of course he's an expert!
29 JENNY: I'd be like this ... *(Turning Barbie's head back and forth)*
30   Then I'd konk him with my teeth. Maybe even bite him, too!
31 BRIANNA: His tongue?
32 JENNY: No! His lip, stupid!
33 BRIANNA: Unless he stuck his tongue ...
34 JENNY: Brianna! I just want a normal kiss that's not with my
35   mirror!

1   BRIANNA: With Jake Daniels ...

2   JENNY: I bet he's kissed lots of girls.

3   BRIANNA: Tons of them. Who would you want to kiss?

4   JENNY: *(Thinking)* Hmmmm ... probably Matt Riley.

5   BRIANNA: Jenny, Matt Riley would never kiss you!

6   JENNY: Gee, thanks, Brianna!

7   BRIANNA: He's like, Mr. Popular at school. And I'm sure he's
8   another expert at kissing.

9   JENNY: Well, if I could choose ...

10 BRIANNA: *(Holds up Ken.)* Oh, Barbie...

11 JENNY: Oh, Ken ... *(Again they struggle with the dolls)* Just kiss
12   me already!

13 BRIANNA: I'm trying! Stop moving your head all around.

14   *(Grabs Barbie and slams them together.)*

15 JENNY: Oh yeah, that was romantic!

16 BRIANNA: *(Throws the dolls down.)* We're too old to play
17   Barbies!

18 JENNY: And old enough to be kissed!

19 BRIANNA: Well, let's clean up this mess and find something
20   more mature to do.

21 JENNY: *(Holding up Barbie)* Oh Ken, will I ever have my first
22   kiss?

23 BRIANNA: Of course you will, Barbie. Pucker up! *(Ken kisses
24   Barbie.)* How was that?

25 JENNY: Not bad.

26 BRIANNA: Not bad?

27 JENNY: It'd be better if it were real.

28 BRIANNA: Pucker up, Jenny. *(Ken kisses JENNY.)*

29 JENNY: Oh, Ken, you are the best kisser! *(They share a laugh.*
30   *NICK, a bit of a nerd, enters.)*

31 NICK: Playing Barbies?

32 BRIANNA: Oh, hey, Nick. Yeah, Jenny and I were trying to relive
33   our childhood.

34 NICK: And did it work?

35 JENNY: It wasn't the same. Ken just isn't enough for me

1   anymore. I need a real man now. *(The girls laugh.)*

2   NICK: Really?

3   BRIANNA: Nick, just out of curiosity ... who was the first girl

4   you kissed?

5   NICK: *(Nervously)* First girl? As in first?

6   BRIANNA: Yeah. Who was the first girl that you kissed?

7   NICK: Well, I ...

8   JENNY: Can you even remember?

9   NICK: Gosh, I can't. It's been so long ago. And there's been so

10   many. *(The girls laugh.)*

11   BRIANNA: Yeah, right.

12   NICK: So, so many.

13   BRIANNA: So you're the expert?

14   NICK: That's me.

15   BRIANNA: Then maybe you could help.

16   NICK: Help?

17   BRIANNA: *(Stands in front of NICK.)* I'm ready to have my first

18   kiss!

19   NICK: *(Voice squeaks)* With me?

20   BRIANNA: You're the expert.

21   NICK: Well, I ... I ... *(Nervously finds lip balm in his pocket, turns*

22   *and thickly applies it.)*

23   BRIANNA: So what do I do?

24   JENNY: *(Stands to help.)* OK, if he turns his head to the right,

25   then you should turn your head to his left.

26   NICK: Wait! I'm going to the right or she's going to the right?

27   BRIANNA: I'm left, right?

28   JENNY: Right! And then you pucker up. That way you don't

29   konk each other's teeth. *(To NICK)* Right?

30   NICK: *(Puckers up.)* Yeah, yeah, that's right. *(Through puckered*

31   *lips)* I'm ready.

32   BRIANNA: But isn't the guy supposed to make the first move?

33   NICK: *(Through puckered lips)* I'm ready.

34   JENNY: Maybe you two can meet in the middle.

35   NICK: OK. *(Closes his eyes and leans forward.)*

1   **BRIANNA:** *(After a long pause of looking at NICK, she shakes her*
2   *head and walks away. NICK doesn't move.)* **I can't do it!**
3   **JENNY: Why not?**
4   **BRIANNA: I'm sorry, but I don't want the memory of my first**
5   **kiss to be with Nick.**
6   **JENNY: But it'd be good practice.**
7   **BRIANNA: Then you practice on him.**
8   **JENNY:** *(Looks back at him.)* **Well ...**
9   **BRIANNA: He's ready.**
10 **JENNY: I don't know. I mean, I guess it'd beat a mirror.**
11 **BRIANNA:** *(Gives her a little push.)* **Then do it!**
12 **JENNY: Maybe ...** *(She approaches NICK slowly.)*
13 **NICK: Hurry up, already. Don't be scared.** *(Slowly, she leans*
14 *forward. He makes kissing sounds.)* **I'm ready for my first**
15 **kiss! I mean, to give you your first kiss.** *(Pause, JENNY looks*
16 *at him. Suddenly, she leans down, picks up the Barbie doll*
17 *and kisses his lips with the doll. Before he can see, she*
18 *quickly places the doll behind her back. He opens his eyes.)*
19 **Oh, I see we did a little switch-a-roo, here. But that's OK.**
20 **BRIANNA: So how did she do, Nick? Did she kiss OK?**
21 **NICK: Jenny, let me assure you, you are a fabulous kisser.**
22 **JENNY:** *(Trying not to laugh)* **I am?**
23 **NICK: The best!**
24 **JENNY: Out of all of the girls you've kissed, I'm the best?**
25 **NICK: The best!** *(Applies more lip balm.)* **So, you want to catch a**
26 **movie this weekend? We can sit in the back and practice ...**
27 **JENNY: Sorry, I can't! I uh ...**
28 **BRIANNA: She has plans with me! Sorry.**
29 **NICK: Oh. OK. Well, maybe some other time.**
30 **JENNY: Maybe.** *(NICK exits, then BRIANNA and JENNY burst into*
31 *laughter.)*
32 **BRIANNA:** *(Picks up Ken.)* **Oh, Barbie ...**
33 **JENNY:** *(Picks up Barbie.)* **Oh, Ken ...** *(The dolls kiss.)*

8. Consolation Prize

CAST: (1M, 3F) ASHLEY, TARA, PENNY, CORY

PROPS: Books.

SETTING: Library.

1　*(At rise TARA, ASHLEY, and PENNY are sitting at a table*
2　*reading. After a moment, TARA glances up, smiles and*
3　*waves.)*
4　**ASHLEY: Tara, who are you waving at?**
5　**TARA:** *(Dreamy tone)* **Cory. He is so amazing.**
6　**ASHLEY: And unavailable.**
7　**TARA: Don't remind me.**
8　**ASHLEY: Unfortunately, Hailey has him in her back pocket.**
9　**TARA: I hope she realizes what a lucky girl she is. How long do**
10　**you think they've been going out?**
11　**ASHLEY: Forever it seems. They've been going out for so long**
12　**that you can't think of Hailey without thinking of Cory. Or**
13　**vice versa.**
14　**TARA: Well, I think Tara and Cory sound better than Hailey and**
15　**Cory. Don't you think?**
16　**ASHLEY: Yes, but what does that matter? Are you going to ask**
17　**him to break up with Hailey because your name has a**
18　**better fit with his?**
19　**TARA: I wish. Or I could try another tactic.**
20　**ASHLEY: Such as?**
21　**TARA: I don't know. Let's see, I could ... throw myself at him?**
22　**ASHLEY:** *(Laughs.)* **Can I watch while you make a fool out of**
23　**yourself? Look, he's coming this way again.**
24　**TARA:** *(Sits up straight and watches him pass, smiling.)* **He didn't**
25　**even look this way.**
26　**ASHLEY: Probably because he's looking for Hailey.**

1 TARA: Probably. So, how can I get him to notice me?

2 ASHLEY: Besides falling at his feet?

3 TARA: Yes, besides that.

4 ASHLEY: I don't know.

5 PENNY: *(Lowers book.)* I have a suggestion.

6 TARA: What?

7 PENNY: Tell him the truth.

8 TARA: What? Just go up to Cory and say, *(Takes Ashley's hand)*

9   "Cory, the truth is, I love you."

10 PENNY: Not that truth.

11 TARA: Then what truth?

12 PENNY: The truth he doesn't know.

13 ASHLEY: The truth he doesn't know?

14 TARA: He doesn't know that I love him.

15 ASHLEY: You don't love him!

16 TARA: Yes I do!

17 ASHLEY: You can't love someone that you barely know.

18 TARA: Oh yes I can! I love Cory! Let me shout it to the world!

19 ASHLEY: *(Patting her hand)* Let's not and say you did.

20 TARA: If it would get his attention, I would.

21 PENNY: Telling him the truth will get his attention.

22 ASHLEY: Penny, what truth are you talking about?

23 PENNY: The truth about her cheating ways.

24 ASHLEY: *(Pointing to TARA)* Hers?

25 TARA: *(Pointing to herself)* Mine?

26 ASHLEY: Does Cory like cheaters?

27 TARA: I haven't cheated! You have to have a boyfriend to cheat!

28 PENNY: Not hers!

29 TARA: Then whose?

30 PENNY: Hailey's. *(Matter of fact)* She's cheating on him.

31 ASHLEY: She is? How do you know?

32 PENNY: Don't ask.

33 TARA: No, you have to tell us! How do you know Hailey is

34   cheating on Cory?

35 ASHLEY: And with who?

44

1 TARA: Yeah, who?

2 PENNY: You didn't hear this from me, OK?

3 TARA: OK!

4 ASHLEY: OK, sure!

5 PENNY: She's cheating with my big brother.

6 ASHLEY: She is?

7 TARA: Oh my gosh!

8 PENNY: Last night, Hailey and my brother were sitting on the
9   front porch swing holding hands and laughing up a
10   storm.

11 ASHLEY: Did you say anything? Like, "Hey, bro, that chick you
12   have your arm around has a boyfriend?"

13 PENNY: Nope. None of my business.

14 TARA: Wow. Why would anyone cheat on Cory? I wouldn't.

15 ASHLEY: Really. Poor Cory.

16 TARA: Yeah. *(Suddenly smiles.)* Yes, it's so sad.

17 ASHLEY: Are you going to tell him?

18 TARA: Yes! No, wait! I can't! I mean, I don't want him to look at
19   me and always associate me with breaking his heart.

20 ASHLEY: But maybe it won't be broken. Maybe he'll say good
21   riddance and be grateful to you for setting him free.

22 TARA: Maybe ...

23 PENNY: Actually, Tara shouldn't be the one to tell him.

24 TARA: *(To ASHLEY)* See! I shouldn't be the one to do it!

25 ASHLEY: Then you should do it, Penny.

26 PENNY: Oh, I can't. I have to live with my brother. I don't want
27   to be caught in the middle of this mess.

28 ASHLEY: Then who should tell him?

29 TARA: Should we send him a note?

30 PENNY: Ashley should tell him.

31 ASHLEY: Me? Why me?

32 PENNY: Because you have no interest in the outcome.

33 ASHLEY: Yes, I do! Because I want my best friend to hook up
34   with Cory so she'll be happy.

35 PENNY: Then you should help your best friend out.

1 TARA: Would you do that for me, Ashley?

2 ASHLEY: Tara, I don't know.

3 TARA: Please!

4 PENNY: Here comes Cory again. *(They ALL sit up and intensely*

5 *watch as CORY walks by. TARA smiles and gives him a small*

6 *wave.)*

7 TARA: He looks sad.

8 ASHLEY: Maybe he already knows.

9 TARA: But maybe you should go over there and tell him just to

10 make sure.

11 ASHLEY: I don't know if I want to do this, Tara.

12 TARA: Ashley, please!

13 ASHLEY: What am I supposed to say? "Uh, Cory, in case you

14 didn't know, Hailey is cheating on you with Penny's

15 brother."

16 PENNY: Leave my name out of it, please.

17 ASHLEY: OK. "Sorry, Cory, but Hailey is cheating on you. What?

18 How do I know? Let me just say I heard it from a good

19 source." *(To PENNY)* You are a good source, aren't you?

20 PENNY: Of course I am. I saw them.

21 ASHLEY: "And Cory, I know this is hard to hear, but if it was me,

22 I'd want to know. Oh, and by the way, my best friend over

23 there wants to know if you'll go out with her."

24 TARA: You can't say that!

25 PENNY: That won't work.

26 ASHLEY: Then what's the point of him finding out about Hailey

27 cheating on him? He needs a reason to notice you.

28 TARA: But not like that!

29 ASHLEY: Then how?

30 TARA: Well, maybe you could invite him over here to sit with us

31 and we can console him. Then, I know! One by one, you

32 two can disappear. Like, "Oh, I've got to run! I forgot I had

33 to do something! Bye!" Then it'll just be me and Cory.

34 *(Smiles.)* Alone at last.

35 PENNY: That's actually not a bad idea.

1   TARA: So go tell him, Ashley!
2   ASHLEY: I don't know, Tara...
3   PENNY: You're the best person to do it.
4   ASHLEY: You're going to owe me for this, Tara.
5   TARA: I'll pay up! You know I will!
6   ASHLEY: *(Stands.)* All right, I'll do it.
7   TARA: Thank you, thank you, thank you!
8   PENNY: Good luck.
9   ASHLEY: *(Walks over to the table where CORY is sitting. He is*
10   *reading a book.)* Hi.
11 CORY: *(Looks up.)* Hi. *(Pause)* You can sit here if you'd like.
12 ASHLEY: Thank you. *(He goes back to his reading. She stares at*
13   *him. Long pause.)*
14 CORY: Did you want to borrow one of my books or something?
15 ASHLEY: No. But thanks.
16 CORY: OK. *(Goes back to his reading. After another long pause, he*
17   *looks at ASHLEY who is still staring at him.)* Is there
18   something you wanted to say?
19 ASHLEY: Yes.
20 CORY: *(After a pause)* Well?
21 ASHLEY: I have to tell you something!
22 CORY: What? Like this is your reserved table in the library and
23   I'm sitting at it?
24 ASHLEY: *(Laughs.)* No, that's not it.
25 CORY: OK. *(Stares at her as he waits. A pause.)* Well?
26 ASHLEY: *(Blurts out.)* Hailey is cheating on you!
27 CORY: She is?
28 ASHLEY: I'm sorry to be the one to tell you! But I thought you
29   should know. I mean, if it were me, I'd want to know. And
30   I'm sure you're really upset and you feel like you could
31   almost cry or something, but my friends and I are sitting
32   over there ... *(Points to their table)* And if you want, you
33   could come over there and sit with us! Maybe we could
34   help you feel better or something. My best friend, Tara,
35   the pretty one over there wearing the *(Change to correct*

1   *color)* **white shirt ... she's really good at consoling people. I**
2   **know, because she's always been there for me. And would**
3   **you believe that she doesn't have a boyfriend? Lucky for**
4   **you, huh? So, do you want to come over there and sit with**
5   **us?** *(Finally takes a deep breath.)*
6 **CORY: So, do you?**
7 **ASHLEY: Do I what?**
8 **CORY: Have a boyfriend?**
9 **ASHLEY: Me? No.** *(After he smiles at her)* **Single and available.**
10   *(Quickly)* **But Tara over there, the cute one wearing the ...**
11 **CORY: White shirt.**
12 **ASHLEY: She's available!**
13 **CORY: But you're not?**
14 **ASHLEY: No.** *(As he is smiling at her)* **I mean, I don't think so. I**
15   **mean, why are you asking?**
16 **CORY: Just wondering if you'd like to hang out sometime.**
17 **ASHLEY: Me? You mean, me and you?**
18 **CORY: Yeah. And I guess you could bring along your friend**
19   **with the white shirt.**
20 **ASHLEY: Oh, no! She wouldn't want to tag along!**
21 **CORY: So, is that a yes?**
22 **ASHLEY: Yes!** *(Quickly)* **Wait, no!**
23 **CORY: What?**
24 **ASHLEY: I can't go!**
25 **CORY: Why not?**
26 **ASHLEY: Because you ...** *(Points to him.)*
27 **CORY: Yes?**
28 **ASHLEY: You need to come over to my table and meet my best**
29   **friend!**
30 **CORY: The one wearing the white shirt?**
31 **ASHLEY: Yes!** *(Stands.)* **OK?**
32 **CORY:** *(Stands.)* **Sure.** *(They go to the other table.)*
33 **ASHLEY: Tara, this is Cory.**
34 **TARA:** *(Gives him a huge smile.)* **Hi!**
35 **CORY: Hey.** *(They ALL sit down.)*

1   TARA: Cory, we're so sorry. But we all agreed you should know
2   the truth about Hailey.
3   PENNY: *(Looks at watch.)* Oh my gosh! Look at the time! I've got
4   to go! Bye! *(Rushes out.)*
5   TARA: When I was in the sixth grade, I caught my boyfriend
6   cheating on me in the lunchroom and it really hurt.
7   CORY: I bet. I'm sorry that happened.
8   TARA: But I believe the best thing you can do is get on with
9   your life and move on as quickly as possible. Heck, when
10   Joey cheated on me, I had a new boyfriend by the end of
11   the day!
12   CORY: Good for you.
13   TARA: *(Stares at ASHLEY.)* Did you say something, Ashley?
14   ASHLEY: No.
15   TARA: Oh. Well, didn't you have a dentist appointment?
16   ASHLEY: No.
17   TARA: You didn't?
18   ASHLEY: No. Oh, oh, oh! I was supposed to go somewhere!
19   Where was I supposed to go?
20   CORY: To hang out with me, remember?
21   TARA: What?
22   CORY: *(To TARA)* But you can tag along if you want.
23   TARA: *What?*
24   CORY: Or I could set you up with one of my friends. Are you OK
25   about blind dates?
26   TARA: *(To CORY)* Wait a minute! Aren't you upset?
27   CORY: I'll be upset if Ashley doesn't hang out with me.
28   TARA: *(As ASHLEY giggles, TARA glares at her.)* No, aren't you
29   upset about Hailey?
30   CORY: Oh, not at all. We broke up last week.
31   TARA: You did?
32   ASHLEY: You did?
33   CORY: *(To TARA)* And several times I've thought about asking
34   your friend out here, but I just didn't have the guts. But
35   when she came over and approached me as a concerned

1   friend ... well, it was like a sign.

2   ASHLEY: *(Gleaming)* A sign?

3   CORY: *(They stare into each other's eyes.)* It was to me.

4   ASHLEY: Really?

5   CORY: I think so. It's almost like you could read my mind.

6   ASHLEY: *(Giggles.)* I couldn't. What were you thinking?

7   CORY: That I wanted to meet you.

8   ASHLEY: I'm glad we met.

9   CORY: Me too.

10   TARA: *(Jumps up.)* Well, gosh, I have to go!

11   ASHLEY: You do?

12   TARA: Yes!

13   ASHLEY: Where are you going?

14   TARA: I don't know! Get a root canal! Go to a funeral! Clean my

15   room!

16   ASHLEY: *(Jumps up.)* Oh, I have to go, too!

17   CORY: Are we still going to get together? Maybe after school?

18   ASHLEY: I'll have to get back to you on that! *(Rushes after TARA.)*

19   Tara, wait!

20   TARA: *(As they exit)* Ashley, what just happened back there? He

21   was supposed to ask me out!

22   ASHLEY: I have no idea! I swear! But you go back over there!

23   I'm leaving!

24   TARA: But he likes you!

25   ASHLEY: And he'll like you once he gets to know you!

26   TARA: Look, Ashley, you tried your best to hook me up with

27   Cory and it didn't work. It's not your fault that he liked

28   you instead of me. That's just the way it goes sometimes.

29   ASHELY: You're not mad?

30   TARA: No, I'm not mad.

31   ASHLEY: Are you sure?

32   TARA: I'm sure. But about me tagging along ...

33   ASHLEY: You're going to tag along?

34   TARA: If he can set me up with one of his friends. But he better

35   not like you better than me!

1 ASHLEY: Are you sure?

2 TARA: I'm sure. We'll just consider his friend my consolation

3   prize.

4 ASHLEY: Hold on. *(Goes to CORY.)* I can do something with you

5   after school.

6 CORY: Great.

7 ASHLEY: And you can find a date for my friend?

8 CORY: You bet! And I have the perfect guy in mind.

9 ASHLEY: Great! See you after school. Bye!

10 CORY: Bye!

11 ASHLEY: *(To TARA)* Cory has the perfect guy for you.

12 TARA: He does? Who?

13 ASHLEY: He didn't say.

14 TARA: Maybe it's Ryan! Or Blake! Or it could be Mitchell or

15   Daniel or Jason, or ...

16 ASHLEY: Come on, let's get to class!

17 TARA: Maybe he has a twin brother.

18 ASHLEY: I don't think so.

19 TARA: Or an older brother.

20 ASHLEY: I have no idea.

21 TARA: Well, as long as he's cute. Well, he doesn't have to be that

22   cute, but he has to be nice. What do you think he looks

23   like?

24 ASHLEY: I don't know, Tara. But we'll find out in a couple of

25   hours.

26 TARA: I hope its Ryan. But Bobby or Tyler would be OK, too.

27 ASHLEY: Come on! *(Pulls her offstage.)*

9. Thirty Days to a New Teen

CAST: (2M, 3F) JASON, TIM, CASSIE, KAREN, LACY
PROPS: Notebooks or backpacks.
SETTING: School hallway.

1 JASON: Hey, Tim, what's up?

2 TIM: Good afternoon, Mr. Williams.

3 JASON: Mr. Williams?

4 TIM: Mr. Williams, I'm in dire need of your help.

5 JASON: No problem, but you need to drop the Mr. Williams!

6 TIM: My sincerest apologies.

7 JASON: What is wrong with you? You're acting like a polite alien

8   from outer space.

9 TIM: Again, I apologize.

10 JASON: Stop it! Just tell me what's going on!

11 TIM: I'm afraid you won't believe me.

12 JASON: Look, Tim, I've been in my share of messes. You know

13   that first hand. So lay it on me and I'll do my best to help

14   you take care of whatever it is you did. And we definitely

15   want to do that before your parents find out.

16 TIM: Oh, they know.

17 JASON: Damn!

18 TIM: Mr. Williams, that is not an acceptable word.

19 JASON: What? Damn? I say it all the time! Damn, damn, damn!

20   Lighten up, Tim! So, back to what you did ... let's start at

21   the beginning.

22 TIM: Well ...

23 CASSIE: *(Enters.)* Hey, Tim, can I borrow your notes for Friday's

24   history test?

1   TIM: Yes, ma'am. *(Finds notes and hands them to her.)* **It is my**
2   **pleasure to loan these notes to you.**
3   CASSIE: *(Smiles.)* **Wow, you're being awfully polite today. Thank**
4   **you!**
5   TIM: You're welcome.
6   CASSIE: Oh, and is it all right if I keep these until tomorrow? I
7   missed some of the notes since I wasn't in class yesterday.
8   TIM: Yes, ma'am.
9   CASSIE: Great! Well, thank you very much, sir!
10   TIM: You're very welcome, Miss Hill. *(CASSIE exits.)*
11   JASON: Tim, what is wrong with you? Are you trying out some
12   new polite and respectful personality? Because let me tell
13   you, it's not cool. In fact, it's downright irritating!
14   TIM: Mr. Williams, that's what I've been trying to tell you! It's
15   why I need your help!
16   JASON: Is this a joke?
17   TIM: No, sir!
18   JASON: You're actually serious?
19   TIM: Yes, sir!
20   JASON: Yes, sir? No, sir? What's wrong with you, Tim?
21   KAREN: *(Enters)* Hey, Tim, I was looking for you.
22   TIM: Good morning, Miss Jones.
23   KAREN: Miss Jones?
24   JASON: Tim is wearing his polite hat today.
25   TIM: I'm not wearing a hat.
26   KAREN: Oh. Well, I was wondering if you wanted to walk over
27   to the Snow Cone Palace after school with me and Jessica.
28   Because I know you have a little crush thing going on with
29   her.
30   TIM: Thank you, Miss Jones. I'd be delighted.
31   KAREN: Delighted?
32   JASON: He meant stoked, pumped, ready to go! Right, Tim?
33   TIM: Yes, sir.
34   KAREN: Well, I like your new polite attitude. In fact, I think
35   most girls would find it quite charming.

1 JASON: I doubt that.

2 KAREN: Because there are hardly any gentlemen left these
3   days.

4 JASON: Because it's old-fashioned.

5 KAREN: And I think you should try your new manners out on
6   Jessica this afternoon.

7 JASON: I wouldn't do that, Tim. Trust me.

8 KAREN: Well, I've got to run. Meet us at the band hall when the
9   bell rings, OK? Oh, and you can come too, Jason!

10 JASON: Gee, thanks.

11 TIM: *(Waves.)* Good-bye, Miss Jones! I'll see you after school!

12 JASON: *(Jerks his hand down.)* Stop it! Now for the last time, tell
13   me what has happened to my good friend, Tim!

14 TIM: Mr. Williams ...

15 JASON: And don't call me Mr. Williams!

16 TIM: I apologize.

17 JASON: And don't apologize!

18 TIM: I'm sorry.

19 JASON: Stop it! Now just tell me what happened to you!

20 TIM: My mother did this.

21 JASON: Your mother did this?

22 TIM: Yes, sir.

23 JASON: And stop saying, "Yes, sir!"

24 TIM: I'm sorry, Mr. Williams.

25 JASON: Tim, what has she done to you?

26 TIM: My mother ordered this program over the Internet.

27 JASON: What program?

28 TIM: A program called, "Thirty Days to a New Teen."

29 JASON: Oh, damn!

30 TIM: There were CDs, books and videos ... and everyday and
31   every night ...

32 JASON: Oh, double damn!

33 TIM: I think my mother even turned them on while I was
34   sleeping. And this morning I woke up and, well ... see what
35   has happened?

1 JASON: You've been brainwashed!
2 TIM: Mr. Williams, could you please help me?
3 JASON: This is bad! This is really, really bad!
4 TIM: Please, Mr. Williams!
5 JASON: This is going to be tough! But you know what? I'm up
6   for the challenge!
7 TIM: Thank you.
8 JASON: Can you meet me back here during lunch? That'll give
9   me time to figure out how to undo the brainwashing your
10   mother has inflicted on you.
11 TIM: Yes, sir, I can meet you at lunch.
12 JASON: OK, good. And until then, try not to talk to anyone, OK?
13 TIM: Yes, sir.
14 JASON: Especially the jocks! Dang, they might even beat you
15   up! I know, act like you have laryngitis.
16 TIM: Laryngitis?
17 JASON: Yeah! Unless you want to die! So meet me back here at
18   lunch! And don't talk to anyone! *(THEY exit. After a*
19   *moment, TIM enters alone. He looks at his watch, and then*
20   *looks around. CASSIE enters.)*
21 CASSIE: Hi, Tim. *(TIM waves.)* Are you meeting someone for
22   lunch? *(TIM nods.)* Who are you meeting?
23 TIM: Mr. Williams.
24 CASSIE: Oh, I see you're still doing the polite thing. *(TIM nods.)*
25   I like it. It reminds me of the old movies I watch
26   sometimes. You know, where the girls are all ladylike and
27   the men are such gentlemen, arriving with flowers and
28   opening doors. *(TIM nods.)* But nowadays the guys can be
29   like, "What are you staring at? Hey, you can open your own
30   door! You ain't no weakling!" *(TIM nods.)* So, don't you
31   change a bit. I like it! See ya later. *(She exits. TIM waves*
32   *good-bye and looks at his watch. LACY enters, dropping*
33   *something as she passes by. TIM rushes to pick it up for her.)*
34 TIM: Excuse me! Ma'am! I believe you dropped something!
35 LACY: *(Turns.)* Oh, thank you! But ... did you just call me

1   ma'am?

2 TIM: Yes, ma'am!

3 LACY: Are you like a student teacher or something? But you

4   don't look old enough to be a student teacher.

5 TIM: No, ma'am. I'm just a student.

6 LACY: Oh. *(Looks around.)* Are you in trouble? I mean, did you

7   get thrown out of class? And you have to stand here until

8   you've learned a little respect! I bet it was Mr. Skinner,

9   wasn't it? He is so uptight! *(Looks around.)* He's watching

10   you, isn't he?

11 TIM: No, ma'am. No one is watching me. And Mr. Skinner

12   didn't throw me out of class.

13 LACY: You're not a foreign exchange student, are you?

14 TIM: No, ma'am.

15 LACY: I didn't think so. I thought I'd seen you around here

16   before. So, what's up with the "no, ma'am" and "yes,

17   ma'am" stuff? Have you been like, brainwashed by your

18   parents?

19 TIM: Yes, ma'am, I believe I have.

20 LACY: Are you serious?

21 TIM: Yes, ma'am.

22 LACY: What did they do? Beat you up every time you weren't

23   polite?

24 TIM: No, ma'am. But my mother did make me listen to a series

25   of tapes called, "Thirty Days to a New Teen."

26 LACY: I've heard of that! My parents were watching that

27   infomercial last night on TV!

28 TIM: Uh-oh.

29 LACY: And Mom was sitting there nodding her head and I made

30   some comment like, "What kind of idiot parent would

31   order that?"

32 TIM: That may not have been a wise thing to say, Miss ... Miss ...

33 LACY: Edwards. But you can call me Lacy ... that is, if you can.

34   Oh, and then my dad glared at me and ordered me to take

35   the trash out and you know what I said?

1 **TIM: Yes, sir?**

2 **LACY: No, I said, "I'll get around to it."**

3 **TIM: Did you?**

4 **LACY: Are you serious? I'm not taking out the trash! Unless I'm**

5   **absolutely forced to!** *(Suddenly)* **Oh, no!**

6 **TIM: What?**

7 **LACY: This morning before school my mom was so happy. She**

8   **was saying things like, "Things are about to change**

9   **around here, Missy." I was like, "Whatever." Do you think**

10   **... do you suppose ...**

11 **TIM: Yes, ma'am, I'm afraid so. That infomercial worked on my**

12   **parents. And see what has happened to me?**

13 **LACY: Oh, no!**

14 **TIM: I thought I was doing OK, until my mom forced me to**

15   **listen to them at night. That's the kicker. You think you're**

16   **asleep and some voice is talking to your subconscious all**

17   **night long.**

18 **LACY: You've been brainwashed!** *(TIM nods.)* **And I might be next!**

19 **TIM: Miss Edwards, if you'd like, my friend Jason is meeting me**

20   **here shortly with a plan to undo my brainwashing.**

21   **Perhaps you would like to stay and hear his plan in case**

22   **your parents have ordered that program.**

23 **LACY: You bet I will! There's no way I'm letting my parents**

24   **brainwash me into becoming some polite teen!**

25 **TIM:** *(Looks at his watch.)* **Jason should be here any minute now.**

26 **LACY: I hope he has a surefire plan, don't you?**

27 **TIM: Yes, ma'am.**

28 **JASON:** *(Enters carrying several papers in a folder.)* **Tim, relax.**

29   **I'm here with a plan to deprogram you!** *(Notices LACY.)*

30 **LACY: Hi. I'm Lacy. Uh, I think my parents have ordered the**

31   **same program and I'm here to avoid any brainwashing**

32   **tactics they may attempt.**

33 **JASON: Oh, good, good.** *(Pulls out his notes.)* **OK, the first thing**

34   **you need to do is realize you're a survivor. You need to step**

35   **back and believe that everything you have been told is a**

1   lie.

2   LACY: It's all a lie.

3   TIM: All a lie.

4   JASON: *(Reading his notes)* And as a survivor, you have suffered
5   the most horrific and despicable crimes against
6   humanity.

7   TIM: I have?

8   JASON: *(Reading)* And the true and real person that you are is
9   what has kept you alive. And now as you go through the
10   process of deprogramming, you will have a better life. So
11   first, realize that you can never trust a programmer.

12 TIM: The videos and CDs?

13 JASON: No, your mother! You can't trust her.

14 TIM: I can't trust my mother?

15 JASON: Absolutely not! *(Reading)* She will always tell you lies!
16   Even when she is telling you the truth.

17 LACY: That doesn't make sense.

18 JASON: Well, that's what it says! *(Looking at notes)* Your mother
19   is selfish in wanting you to do criminal activities.

20 TIM: Being polite is a criminal activity?

21 JASON: Yes! To teenagers it is! *(Looking at notes)* You need not
22   buy into the lies that are told to you by the cult.

23 LACY: The cult?

24 JASON: His family! *(Looking at notes)* The core stages are heavy
25   and continual torture.

26 TIM: I haven't been tortured!

27 JASON: Destroying your trust and demanding obedience.

28 LACY: The obedience thing is correct.

29 JASON: So you, the survivor, need to go back to the trauma ...

30 TIM: There was no trauma.

31 JASON: So you can dismantle the system ... deflate the layers ...

32 LACY: Huh?

33 JASON: So you ... uh ... can be in touch with your own emotions
34   and be responsible for them.

35 TIM: So what do I do?

1 JASON: *(Puts notes aside.)* **Let's practice.**
2 TIM: **Practice?**
3 JASON: **Work with me. Let's just try this. Pretend I'm your**
4   **mom.**
5 TIM: *(Reluctantly)* **OK ...**
6 LACY: **Maybe I should be the mom.**
7 JASON: **No, you need to pay attention.**
8 LACY: **OK.**
9 JASON: **Tim, would you please set the table for dinner?**
10 TIM: **Yes, ma'am.**
11 JASON: **No! No! Try it again! Tim, would you please set the table**
12   **for dinner?**
13 LACY: *(Nudges him)* **Say no.**
14 TIM: **No, ma'am.**
15 JASON: **Well, that's better, but try leaving out the ma'am part.**
16   **Try it again. Tim, would you please set the table for**
17   **dinner?**
18 TIM: *(Looks at LACY, then JASON. A pause, then suddenly)* **No!**
19 JASON: *(Claps his hands together.)* **Great! Let's try something**
20   **else. Tim, would you take out the trash for me?**
21 TIM: **No!**
22 JASON: **Clean your room?**
23 TIM: **No!**
24 JASON: **Do your homework?**
25 TIM: **No! No, I won't!**
26 LACY: **You did it, Jason! You've deprogrammed him!**
27 JASON: **Yes, I did! It was hard, but I believe I have been**
28   **successful.**
29 LACY: **But what do I do if my parents come home with that**
30   **infomercial product?**
31 JASON: **Refuse to listen to it!**
32 LACY: **And if they make me?**
33 JASON: **Tune it out! And if worse comes to worse and you find**
34   **yourself acting all respectful, then come see me. I can take**
35   **care of it.**

1   LACY: Thanks!

2   JASON: No problem.

3   TIM: Excuse me for interrupting, but I'm getting hungry.

4   JASON: Yeah, me too! Who wants to grab a burger?

5   LACY: Count me in!

6   JASON: Then let's go! Hey, Tim, I think you owe me lunch. You
7   gonna buy me a burger for all the deprogramming that I
8   did on you today?

9   TIM: Yes, sir. I'd be very pleased to pay for your lunch today, Mr.
10   Williams. Shall we leave? Oh, after you, Miss Edwards.

11 JASON: Damn!

12 LACY: I'm running away from home!

10. Be My Valentine

CAST: (3M, 1F) BEN, PHIL, DARREN, ALLISON
PROPS: A note, a single rose.
SETTING: Classroom. Cafeteria.

1 **BEN:** *(Sits at desk, concentrating. Writes, crumples paper and*
2 *throws it on the floor. Begins again.)* **Allison ... Will you be**
3 **my valentine?** *(Crumples paper, throws it on the floor.)*
4 **Allison, this may be a silly question, but ...** *(Crumples*
5 *paper, throws it on the floor)* **Allison, Valentines Day is a**
6 **symbol of love and I thought it was the perfect time to tell**
7 **you ...** *(Crumples paper.)*
8 **PHIL:** *(Enters.)* **Whoa! What's this? Writer's block?**
9 **BEN: You could say that.**
10 **PHIL:** *(Picks up a crumpled paper and reads.)* **Will you be my**
11 **valentine? Did you actually write this?**
12 **BEN:** *(Sarcastically)* **No! I just crumpled up someone else's**
13 **paper!**
14 **PHIL: That's good to hear because this is so lame!**
15 **BEN: Really?**
16 **PHIL: Will you be my valentine? That is so elementary!**
17 **Remember those dorky cards we used to hand out?**
18 **BEN: I thought they were pretty cool. Last year, I had these**
19 **Spider-Man cards and ...**
20 **PHIL: Last year?**
21 **BEN: Well, maybe it wasn't last year. I don't exactly remember.**
22 **Maybe it was a few years ago.**
23 **PHIL: Let's hope so. But nowadays, if you want to impress a girl,**
24 **you have to buy her a dozen roses and a box of chocolates.**
25 **BEN: Dang! Who has money for that? I thought I'd just write**
26 **Allison a heartfelt letter and give her a box of those little**

1   candy hearts. You know, the ones that have a message on
2   each piece of candy. And I also thought I might find one of
3   those little hearts that said "Be Mine" and tape it to my
4   letter. What do you think?
5 PHIL: I think you need to ask your parents for a loan and get a
6   dozen roses and a box of chocolates.
7 BEN: For a girl who may not even want to be my valentine?
8 PHIL: Make it two dozen roses and the biggest box of candy you
9   can find and I'm sure she'll say yes.
10 BEN: But that's a lot of money.
11 PHIL: Question. Is she worth it?
12 BEN: Is she worth it? Allison is worth every rose in the
13   universe.
14 PHIL: Wow! You should write that down.
15 BEN: You think?
16 PHIL: It gives me goose bumps and I'm not even a girl!
17 BEN: Good idea. *(Writes.)* But I know my parents won't give me
18   a loan for a dozen roses, plus there's no time. But maybe
19   ... maybe I can run to the flower shop during lunch and
20   buy her a single rose.
21 PHIL: That might work.
22 BEN: *(Writing)* Allison, this rose is a symbol ...
23 PHIL: Of my love!
24 BEN: That's too direct. I need to ease into this.
25 PHIL: I know! Allison, this rose is just the beginning ...
26 BEN: *(Writing)* Just the beginning ...
27 PHIL: Of the roses you will receive from me ...
28 BEN: *(Writing furiously)* You will receive from me ...
29 PHIL: Because you deserve every rose in the universe ...
30 BEN: *(Writing)* Every rose in the universe ...
31 PHIL: And from this day forward ...
32 BEN: *(Writing)* From this day forward ...
33 PHIL: I will present you with a single rose every single day ...
34 BEN: *(Writing)* Every single day ... *(Looks up)* Wait! I can't afford
35   that!

1   PHIL: You could get a job.

2   BEN: Let's back up. *(Reading)* "Because you deserve every rose
3   in the universe ... "

4   PHIL: Which I'd buy for you if I could.

5   BEN: Yeah! *(Writes.)* Which I'd buy for you if I could ...

6   PHIL: Because you, Allison, are like a rose ...

7   BEN: *(Writes.)* You are like a rose ...

8   PHIL: Soft.

9   BEN: *(Writes.)* Soft.

10 PHIL: Sweet.

11 BEN: *(Writes.)* Sweet.

12 PHIL: Tender.

13 BEN: *(Writes.)* Tender.

14 PHIL: And your breath is as pure as a rose.

15 BEN: *(Looks at Phil.)* But I've never smelled her breath.

16 PHIL: Maybe you did when you talked to her.

17 BEN: But I've never talked to her.

18 PHIL: Never?

19 BEN: No. But I see her around. You know ... in the halls.

20 PHIL: You mean, you don't even know her?

21 BEN: I know her! Well, from a distance.

22 PHIL: *(Takes a deep breath.)* This is going to be harder than I
23   thought.

24 DARREN: *(Enters.)* Hey, what's up?

25 PHIL: Ben's in love with a girl he doesn't know.

26 DARREN: Cool.

27 BEN: I didn't say I was in love!

28 PHIL: No, but you want Allison to be your valentine and you
29   want to give her every rose in the universe.

30 DARREN: Man, you've got it bad!

31 PHIL: I think you should talk to her first.

32 DARREN: You haven't talked to her?

33 BEN: No, not exactly. But she is the most beautiful girl I've ever
34   seen! *(Looking at PHIL)* Gorgeous brown eyes. Glistening
35   hair. That gentle, sweet smile. And yes, she does deserve

1   every rose in the universe!

2   PHIL: Stop that! You're giving me chill bumps again!

3   DARREN: Dang, you're giving me chill bumps, too!

4   BEN: So what do I give her? The handwritten note? The single

5   rose? A box of candy hearts? All of the above? None of the

6   above?

7   PHIL: You should talk to her first, Ben.

8   BEN: I know, but I'm nervous about it.

9   DARREN: No, I don't think you should talk to her first.

10   BEN: You don't?

11   DARREN: No, because it'll ruin the mystery. Not to mention the

12   surprise.

13   BEN: What surprise? That she gets a single red rose and gushy

14   love letter from a complete stranger?

15   DARREN: No! The surprise of a singing telegram from a secret

16   admirer!

17   PHIL: Hey, that's a great idea! Girls like stupid stuff like that.

18   BEN: Yeah! That is a great idea! But who could I get to do it?

19   DARREN: I'll volunteer!

20   PHIL: Volunteer, or does he have to pay you?

21   DARREN: Ben, you don't have to pay me. We'll just say that you

22   owe me one, OK?

23   BEN: Sure, sure, no problem.

24   DARREN: So where should I track her down and present her

25   with the singing telegram?

26   BEN: Well, how about in the cafeteria during lunch?

27   DARREN: That works for me.

28   PHIL: What are you going to sing?

29   DARREN: I don't know. I'll think of something.

30   BEN: Something about me being in love with her, OK?

31   DARREN: Of course.

32   BEN: *(Quickly signs note, folds it and hands it to DARREN.)* And

33   when you finish, give her this note, OK?

34   DARREN: Sure. You think you ought to give her your phone

35   number, too? In case she wants to call you tonight?

1 BEN: *(Takes note and writes.)* **Yeah, good idea.**
2 PHIL: **And if she doesn't call, well, then you'll know.**
3 BEN: **Know what?**
4 PHIL: **She's not interested.**
5 DARREN: **Oh, she'll be interested. How can she not be after her**
6   **singing telegram?** *(Pats BEN on the shoulder.)* **She'll think**
7   **you are the most romantic guy in the world!**
8 PHIL: **What about the rose?**
9 BEN: **Oh yeah.**
10 DARREN: **I know! A single rose, right?**
11 BEN: **Yeah.**
12 DARREN: **Well, Mrs. Johnson received a dozen roses this**
13   **morning in my English class and I bet I could borrow one.**
14 PHIL: **Borrow one? You mean, steal?**
15 DARREN: **Oh, come on. She'll never miss it.**
16 PHIL: **You better hope not.**
17 BEN: **Phil, it's for a worthy cause!**
18 DARREN: **OK, here's the plan. Be in the cafeteria during lunch.**
19 BEN: **OK.**
20 DARREN: **You point her out to me, and then I'll take care of the**
21   **rest. A song, a rose, a note.**
22 PHIL: **This ought to be interesting.**
23 BEN: **Oh, I hope she likes it!**
24 DARREN: **She'll love it! Believe me.**
25 BEN: **OK. See you at lunch.** *(They ALL exit. ALLISON sits at a*
26   *table in the lunchroom. After a moment, BEN, PHIL and*
27   *DARREN enter, all looking her way and nudging each other*
28   *and pointing. DARREN holds a single rose. BEN and PHIL sit*
29   *down, and then DARREN approaches ALLISON.)*
30 DARREN: **For you.** *(Hands her the rose.)*
31 ALLISON: **Why?**
32 DARREN: **Also for you.** *(Hands her the note.)*
33 ALLISON: *(Opens the note and reads.)* **Who's Ben?** *(DARREN*
34   *points across the room. When he does, BEN, embarrassed,*
35   *attempts to hide behind PHIL.)*

1   **ALLISON:** *(Looks at the note again.)* **Every rose in the universe?**

2   **DARREN: Romantic huh? Wait! That's not all!** *(Gets down on*

3   *one knee and begins to sing badly.)* **"When I fall in love, it**

4   **will be forever!" Gosh, I can't remember the rest of it.**

5   **Wait! Let me start over. "When I fall in love, it will be**

6   **forever!" Wait! What is the rest of it? "When I fall in love,**

7   **it will be forever."***(Makes up the rest.)* **"When I fall in love,**

8   **it will be forever! And on this special day, I have a special**

9   **request! Oh, Allison, Allison. *Will you be my valentine?"***

10 **ALLISON:** *(Gives him a strange look.)* **Be your valentine or his**

11   **valentine?** *(Points to Ben who quickly ducks behind PHIL*

12   *again.)*

13 **DARREN:** *(Stands up)* **His!** *(Points to BEN who is peeking around*

14   *PHIL's shoulder.)*

15 **ALLISON:** *(Short pause. She smiles.)* **Yes.**

16 **DARREN: Yes?**

17 **ALLISON: Yes.**

18 **DARREN: Great! Great! Oh, and he put his phone number on**

19   **that note so you can call him tonight, OK?**

20 **ALLISON: OK.** *(Gathers her things. Looks toward BEN, smiles,*

21   *then exits.)*

22 **DARREN:** *(Goes to PHIL and BEN.)* **OK, so my singing wasn't that**

23   **great, but ...**

24 **BEN: What'd she say? What'd she say?**

25 **PHIL: Yeah, what'd she say?**

26 **DARREN: Good news, Ben. She wants to be your valentine.**

27 **BEN: She does?**

28 **DARREN: She does!**

29 **BEN: Yes!**

30 **DARREN: And she'll be calling you tonight.**

31 **BEN: Yes!**

32 **PHIL: So are you going to get a job now?**

33 **BEN: A job?**

34 **PHIL: So you can buy her every rose in the universe?**

35 **DARREN: Or I could give her a singing telegram everyday if you**

1   **wanted. That was fun. But I need to practice.** *(Singing)*
2   **"When I fall in love, it will be forever ... " What is the rest**
3   **of that song? "When I fall in love ... "** *(They ALL exit as*
4   *DARREN continues to sing.)*

11. Imaginary Pets

CAST: (2M, 2F) BILLY, WES, AMY, RENE
PROPS: Books, dictionary.
SETTING: A school library.

1   *(At rise BILLY, WES, AMY and RENE are at a table reading.)*

2   **BILLY:** *(Glances up and looks down.)* **No, no ... you have to be**

3   **quiet.**

4   **WES: Who? Me?**

5   **AMY: Who's not being quiet?**

6   **RENE: I'm being quiet. I didn't say a thing.**

7   **WES: Well, I didn't say anything.**

8   **AMY: Well, someone did.**

9   **RENE: Not me.**

10 **WES: Billy, who were you telling to be quiet?**

11 **BILLY: Relax, relax, it wasn't any of you.**

12 **WES: But who was it?**

13 **BILLY: Someone.**

14 **AMY: Does that someone have a name?**

15 **BILLY: Yes.**

16 **RENE: And is that someone at this table?**

17 **BILLY: Yes.**

18 **WES: Is that someone a girl?**

19 **BILLY: No.**

20 **WES: Then it's me!**

21 **BILLY: No, it's not you, Wes.**

22 **AMY: I know! He's talking to himself!** *(They ALL nod as if this*

23   *makes sense, and then go back to their reading.)*

24 **BILLY:** *(After a pause, he looks down)* **What's wrong? Are you**

25   **hungry?**

26 **WES: Who said they're hungry?**

1   RENE: I'm hungry, but I didn't say it out loud.

2   AMY: I didn't say anything.

3   WES: Billy?

4   BILLY: What?

5   WES: Who were you talking to?

6   BILLY: Someone.

7   AMY: I bet he was talking to his stomach!

8   RENE: Oh, I do that! Mine starts growling in third period and I

9   say, "Shut up, stomach." *(They ALL nod, and then go back to*

10   *their reading.)*

11 BILLY: *(After a pause)* No, no, sit down!

12 WES: What?

13 AMY: Who needs to sit down?

14 WES: No one is standing here, Billy.

15 RENE: Who are you talking to?

16 WES: Maybe it's some mind game he's playing.

17 AMY: That's a weird game.

18 RENE: Oh, I played that before. What you do is stare into

19   someone's eyes and try to figure out what they're thinking.

20   So Billy thought Wes wanted to stand up. Right, Billy?

21 WES: You got that one wrong, Billy. I wasn't thinking about

22   standing up, I was thinking about what I was reading and

23   how I didn't understand it. But good try.

24 AMY: Yeah, good try. *(They ALL go back to their reading.)*

25 BILLY: *(After a pause)* Yes, I love you, too!

26 WES: Who?

27 AMY: *(Points to RENE.)* Her?

28 RENE: Not me! *(Points to AMY.)* Her? You love her?

29 AMY: Not me!

30 RENE: Well, it's not me!

31 WES: Well, don't look at me!

32 AMY: It could be you, Wes. Guys can love each other ... you

33   know, like a brother.

34 WES: Well, let me clue you in, Billy. *(Points finger in his face.)*

35   Don't say that to me again! Unless I croak and you're

1   **trying to deal with your loss!** *(As if crying)* **"I miss you,**

2   **man! You were my best friend! I love you, man!"**

3   **RENE: Wes, you are so stupid.**

4   **WES: Hey, wouldn't you girls cry if I suddenly bit the dust?** *(A*

5   *short pause as the girls look at each other)*

6   **RENE and AMY: No.**

7   **WES: Gee, thanks.** *(They ALL go back to their reading.)*

8   **BILLY:** *(After a pause, speaking baby talk)* **What is it? Huh? What**

9   **is it?**

10 **WES:** *(Pushes his chair back and looks on the floor.)* **What is it?**

11 **AMY:** *(Pushes chair back and looks on the floor.)* **I don't see**

12   **anything.**

13 **RENE:** *(Looks under the table.)* **I don't see anything either.**

14 **WES: Is it a bug?**

15 **AMY:** *(Moves away.)* **A bug?**

16 **RENE:** *(Moves away.)* **I hate bugs!**

17 **BILLY: It's nothing.**

18 **WES: Hey girls, it's nothing.**

19 **RENE: Thank goodness.**

20 **WES: He thought it was something, but it wasn't.** *(They ALL go*

21   *back to their reading.)*

22 **BILLY:** *(After a moment, he looks up.)* **Shhhh ...**

23 **WES: Shhhh? Who? Who's being loud?**

24 **AMY: I didn't say anything.**

25 **RENE: Neither did I.**

26 **WES: Then who are you telling to be quiet?**

27 **RENE: Well, this is a library, Wes.**

28 **WES: I know, Rene, but no one was talking.**

29 **AMY: Well, maybe he was thinking so loud that it sounded like**

30   **someone was talking.**

31 **RENE: I've done that.**

32 **AMY: So I guess he was telling himself to be quiet.** *(They ALL*

33   *nod and go back to their reading.)*

34 **BILLY:** *(After a moment, he looks down.)* **No, no, I can't play right**

35   **now.**

1   **WES:** Play? Play what?

2   **RENE:** I didn't say anything.

3   **AMY:** Me neither.

4   **WES:** Billy?

5   **BILLY:** *(Looking down)* **Get down!** *(WES, AMY and RENE look*

6   *under the table.)* **You've got to be quiet!**

7   **WES:** Who are you talking to?

8   **RENE:** Do you have a pet insect or something?

9   **AMY:** Or an imaginary friend?

10 **BILLY:** How did you know?

11 **AMY:** Know what?

12 **BILLY:** About Bruno.

13 **WES:** Who's Bruno?

14 **AMY:** Is Bruno your imaginary friend?

15 **WES:** You have an imaginary friend?

16 **BILLY:** He is a friend, but actually...

17 **RENE:** What?

18 **BILLY:** He's a dog.

19 **WES:** *(Looks under the table.)* I don't see a dog.

20 **AMY:** That's because he's imaginary, Wes!

21 **RENE:** *(Looking under the table)* **Ahhhh … . What color is he?**

22 **BILLY:** Black with white markings on his paws and ears.

23 **AMY:** Oh, how cute!

24 **WES:** Billy, you're joking, right?

25 **BILLY:** Hey, don't step on his paw!

26 **WES:** *(Jumps up.)* I didn't step on his paw!

27 **AMY:** Wes!

28 **RENE:** How could you do that?

29 **WES:** I didn't? Did I? No, of course I didn't! How can I hurt

30   someone who doesn't exist?

31 **BILLY:** Yes, he does!

32 **WES:** Then why can't I see him?

33 **AMY:** Because you don't have an imaginary bone in your body!

34 **RENE:** Is he OK, Billy?

35 **BILLY:** *(Looking down)* **He's OK.**

1 WES: Hey, can your imaginary dog fetch?

2 BILLY: What?

3 WES: Can he fetch? *(Tosses a pencil across the room.)* **Fetch, Fido!**

4 BILLY: His name is Bruno!

5 WES: Fetch, Bruno! *(Pause as they stare at the pencil.)* **Guess not.**

6 AMY: Maybe he doesn't want to, Wes!

7 RENE: Yeah, and maybe he only takes orders from his master!

8   Billy, can I pet him?

9 BILLY: Sure.

10 WES: *(Laughs.)* If you can find him!

11 RENE: He's right here. *(Pets imaginary dog.)* Isn't that right,

12   Billy? *(Billy nods.)* Oh, you're such a sweet dog!

13 AMY: Let me pet him, too! *(Pets dog.)* Oh, he is sweet!

14 WES: *(Suddenly)* Uh-oh!

15 AMY: What?

16 WES: My imaginary cat is hissing at your dog.

17 RENE: Wes, you don't have a cat!

18 WES: Sure I do. And I hope they don't get into a fight because

19   my cat has these super sharp claws. See?

20 AMY: I don't see a cat.

21 RENE: I don't either.

22 BILLY: Me neither.

23 WES: You don't see my cat, but you see his dog?

24 AMY: Yes!

25 RENE: That's right, Wes. We don't see your cat.

26 WES: *(Looking down, baby talk)* It's all right, little kitty. I see

27   you.

28 AMY: Does your cat have a name?

29 WES: Yes, she does.

30 RENE: And that would be?

31 WES: Kiki.

32 RENE: Kiki?

33 WES: That's right. With huge, super sharp claws! *(Hisses.)* **Did**

34   you hear that?

35 AMY: What I heard was you, Wes.

1 WES: No, no, that was my cat! **Listen!** *(Covers his mouth and*
2   *hisses again.)*
3 **RENE: That was you, Wes.**
4 **BILLY: My dog's not afraid of your cat, Wes.**
5 WES: Well, he should be. 'Cause my cat is mean! *(Hisses.)*
6 **AMY: Oh, no!**
7 **WES: What?**
8 **AMY: I'm sorry, Wes!**
9 **WES: For what? What?**
10 **AMY:** *(Smiles.)* **My coyote just ate your cat.** *(As if petting her*
11   *coyote)* **Were you hungry, Sweetheart?**
12 **WES: Amy, you don't have a coyote!**
13 **AMY: Yes, I do! And your cat ... well, I'm sorry.**
14 **RENE: Want to know what I have?**
15 **WES: What? A stupid parakeet?**
16 **RENE:** *(Proudly)* **I have a monkey!**
17 **WES: A monkey?**
18 **RENE: Yes, and I dress her up and carry her around with me**
19   **everywhere.**
20 **AMY: Ahhhh ... What's her name, Rene?**
21 **RENE: Mitzy.**
22 **AMY: That's a cute name.**
23 **WES:** *(Points to RENE.)* **You don't have a monkey!** *(Points to*
24   *AMY.)* **You don't have a coyote!** *(Points to BILLY.)* **And you**
25   **don't have a dog!**
26 **AMY: And you don't have a cat! Sorry. Nature can be cruel at**
27   **times.**
28 **WES: Can we just lose this conversation over our imaginary**
29   **pets and get back to our reading? Book report in one week,**
30   **people!**
31 **RENE: Fine with me.**
32 **AMY: Yeah, I need to finish this book.** *(They ALL go back to their*
33   *reading.)*
34 **BILLY:** *(Stands, speaking to his dog.)* **Stay.**
35 **WES: Where are you going?**

1 **BILLY: To get a dictionary. I'll be right back.** *(Points to dog.)*
2 **Stay!** *(Exits.)*
3 **AMY: That's right, you're a good boy.**
4 **RENE: He minds well.**
5 **WES: You are all crazy! You know that?**
6 **RENE: Wes, have you not ever had a pet before?**
7 **WES: Sure! One that I could see!**
8 **AMY: And you can't see Bruno?**
9 **WES: No! I see nothing! I see air!**
10 **RENE: You can't see air!**
11 **WES: And you can't see an imaginary pet!**
12 **AMY: Yes, we can.** *(WES shakes his head. They go back to their*
13 *reading. BILLY returns.)*
14 **BILLY:** *(Sits down.)* **Good boy.** *(A pause as they ALL read)*
15 **WES:** *(Jerks his hand back.)* **Stop it!**
16 **BILLY: What's wrong, Wes?**
17 **WES: Someone licked me!**
18 **BILLY: Stop it, Bruno.**
19 **WES:** *(To AMY)* **Did you do that?**
20 **AMY: Uh, no!**
21 **WES:** *(To RENE)* **Did you?**
22 **RENE: No! Gross!** *(WES shakes his head. They continue to read.)*
23 **WES:** *(After a moment, he begins to mumble.)* **I've heard of an**
24 **imaginary friend, but an imaginary pet? And aren't you**
25 **supposed to outgrow that like at the age of five? Are you**
26 **going to take him everywhere with you? Like to college?**
27 **Talk about embarrassing! "But Professor, he's real!"**
28 **Dude, they might just send you to the psycho ward. So, a**
29 **little advice, lose the little invisible pet.**
30 **BILLY:** *(Stands.)* **Bruno ... Sick 'em!**
31 **WES:** *(He bolts out of his chair, jumping up and down.)* **Stop it!**
32 **Stop it! He's biting my ankles! Stop it!** *(Screaming, he runs*
33 *off.)*
34 **BILLY: Good dog.** *(They ALL go back to their reading)*

12. Home Alone

CAST: (2F) ERICA, BROOKE
PROPS: Cell phone.
SETTING: ERICA's bedroom.

1 ERICA: I was thinking ...
2 BROOKE: Uh-oh.
3 ERICA: What if we borrow my mom's car and ...
4 BROOKE: Borrow?
5 ERICA: We'll bring it back!
6 BROOKE: In one piece?
7 ERICA: We borrow my mom's car and ...
8 BROOKE: We?
9 ERICA: I borrow my mom's car and ...
10 BROOKE: Wait! You don't have a driver's license!
11 ERICA: So, we'll take the back roads and be careful not to get
12   caught, head to Jake's and ...
13 BROOKE: Erica, have you taken Driver's Ed?
14 ERICA: Brooke, what do you think? So, anyway, here's what I
15   thought we'd do ...
16 BROOKE: Wait! Do you even know how to drive?
17 ERICA: Of course I do! My papa used to take me out on the
18   country roads.
19 BROOKE: The country roads? Where there are no traffic
20   signals and you just weave all over the place?
21 ERICA: I didn't weave all over the place! I'd sit in Papa's lap and
22   he'd let me steer and ...
23 BROOKE: See, you don't know how to drive!
24 ERICA: Brooke, don't you trust me?
25 BROOKE: No!
26 ERICA: Thanks a lot!

1 BROOKE: Come on, Erica! You've never driven a car in your
2   life! Steering and figuring out if to push the brake or the
3   gas is not that easy.
4 ERICA: So you're not in this with me?
5 BROOKE: I'm sorry, Erica, but I don't want to die.
6 ERICA: Fine! Fine! So it's another boring Friday night. Even my
7   parents are out having fun and what are we doing?
8   Nothing! Zilch!
9 BROOKE: We could walk to Jake's.
10 ERICA: I don't want to walk two miles to Jake's!
11 BROOKE: You wanted to go a minute ago.
12 ERICA: When I thought I could drive!
13 BROOKE: So, we'll think of something else to do.
14 ERICA: Your turn. You think of something.
15 BROOKE: OK. *(Pause)* Play with the hamsters? Maybe build
16   them a little house out of Popsicle sticks?
17 ERICA: Brooke! I want to do something fun and daring, like
18   borrow my mom's car and you want to build a hamster
19   house out of Popsicle sticks? Can't you think of something
20   a bit more exciting than that?
21 BROOKE: Well ...
22 ERICA: *(After a short pause)* Well?
23 BROOKE: Prank phone calls?
24 ERICA: Caller ID!
25 BROOKE: From Jeremy's phone?
26 ERICA: You have Jeremy's phone?
27 BROOKE: *(Takes phone from pocket.)* He asked me to hold it for
28   him and I forgot to give it back.
29 ERICA: Give me that! *(Grabs phone and dials.)*
30 BROOKE: Who are you calling?
31 ERICA: I'm just punching random numbers. Who cares who
32   answers? *(Listens into the phone.)*
33 BROOKE: What are you going to say?
34 ERICA: *(In a mature voice)* Yes, I'd like to order a large
35   pepperoni pizza.

1 BROOKE: You're ordering pizza?

2 ERICA: *(To BROOKE)* **Shhhh!** *(Into phone)* **I have the wrong**

3 **number? ... Are you sure ... You are? Well, could you make**

4 **a pizza and deliver it to my house anyway? ... You won't? ...**

5 **But please! But I'm so hungry! I'm starving! ... Because my**

6 **parents never feed me! ... Call Child Protective Services? ...**

7 **But I'm calling you! ... 911? For Pizza? Hello? Hello?** *(Closes*

8 *phone.)* **She hung up on me.**

9 BROOKE: **Imagine that.**

10 ERICA: *(Dials again.)* **Just random numbers here.** *(Listens into*

11 *the phone.)* **No answer.**

12 BROOKE: **That person is probably out having fun tonight, too.**

13 **Now what?**

14 ERICA: **I don't know.**

15 BROOKE: **Watch TV?**

16 ERICA: **Boring.**

17 BROOKE: **Throw a wild party?**

18 ERICA: **Who would we invite?**

19 BROOKE: **My cousin Mike would probably come.**

20 ERICA: **Brooke, your cousin Mike is ten years old!**

21 BROOKE: **And my sister ...**

22 ERICA: **She's the same age! Do we want to baby-sit or have a**

23 **wild party?**

24 BROOKE: **Erica, most everyone I know already had plans for**

25 **tonight. We could pretend we're having a wild party.**

26 ERICA: **How?**

27 BROOKE: **Turn up the music. Eat lots of food. Run through the**

28 **house and act crazy.**

29 ERICA: **With each other?**

30 BROOKE: **It's just an idea.**

31 ERICA: **Let's think of something else.**

32 BROOKE: **OK. Any ideas.**

33 ERICA: *(Yawns.)* **I'm thinking.**

34 BROOKE: *(Yawns.)* **Call someone?**

35 ERICA: **More prank calls?**

1   BROOKE: No. *(Yawns.)* We could call some friends.

2   ERICA: Who?

3   BROOKE: I don't know.

4   ERICA: Me neither.

5   BROOKE: *(Yawns.)* Walk to the convenience store and buy
6   candy?

7   ERICA: *(Yawns.)* We could.

8   BROOKE: *(Yawns.)* Or we could cook something.

9   ERICA: *(Yawns.)* I guess. Maybe a frozen pizza?

10   BROOKE: Yeah. *(Yawns.)* Or ...

11   ERICA: Or?

12   BROOKE: *(Yawns.)* Or we could put on our P.J.'s and go to bed.

13   ERICA: *(Yawns.)* That's the best idea I've heard. I'm tired.

14   BROOKE: Me too.

15   ERICA: And next Friday night we'll do something fun.

16   BROOKE: Yeah, like throw a wild party.

17   ERICA: The wildest! *(They both yawn.)* Let's go to bed.

18   BROOKE: I'm right behind you.

13. Cookie Dough

CAST: (2M, 2F, 8 Extras, doubling if desired)
DAVID, ERIC, RACHEL, ALYSSA
PROPS: Old shirt with holes, empty can,
newspaper, cash, coins.

1   DAVID: Hey, you didn't show up at the skate park last night.
2   What happened?
3   ERIC: I got grounded.
4   DAVID: Again?
5   ERIC: Yep.
6   DAVID: What did you do this time?
7   ERIC: Nothing major if you ask me!
8   DAVID: So what's the crime? Failing grades? Not cleaning your
9   room? Wait! I know! Having no respect for authority!
10 ERIC: Hey, I have respect for authority!
11 DAVID: So what did you do?
12 ERIC: I ate cookie dough.
13 DAVID: What?
14 ERIC: You heard me right. I ate cookie dough!
15 DAVID: And you're not allowed to eat cookie dough at your
16   house?
17 ERIC: No, it's not that. See, my stupid sister is selling cookie
18   dough as a fundraiser for her stupid pep squad.
19 DAVID: And you ate without paying?
20 ERIC: Let's just say I sampled four different rolls of cookie
21   dough. There was the chocolate chip, double fudge,
22   peanut butter and oatmeal raisin. Except for the oatmeal
23   raisin, they were all pretty good.
24 DAVID: So just pay your sister for the cookie dough.
25 ERIC: She'd already sold them to customers who'd paid up front.

1 DAVID: So give the customers their money back.

2 ERIC: I don't have that much money!

3 DAVID: How much did it cost?

4 ERIC: Forty-eight dollars. Plus tax.

5 DAVID: Forty-eight dollars? For cookie dough?

6 ERIC: I know! It's expensive, isn't it? And the problem is, I don't

7   have forty-eight dollars. Heck, I don't even have forty-

8   eight cents!

9 DAVID: Yikes.

10 ERIC: And my stupid sister was running through the house last

11   night screaming and crying. *(Imitates.)* "Mom, Eric ate my

12   cookie dough! He ate my cookie dough! How can I give our

13   neighbors their cookie dough that's already half eaten?

14   Mom! Mom! Mom!"

15 DAVID: Dang!

16 ERIC: And then, to top all that off, I get this stupid lecture

17   about eating raw eggs.

18 DAVID: You ate raw eggs?

19 ERIC: No, I ate cookie dough!

20 DAVID: But you just said ...

21 ERIC: Mom said there are raw eggs in cookie dough.

22 DAVID: I didn't know that.

23 ERIC: Apparently there is.

24 DAVID: So?

25 ERIC: One word. Salmonella.

26 DAVID: Salmon who?

27 ERIC: Salmonella. Some nasty bacteria that lurks in raw eggs.

28   As mom said, "It's unsafe to eat anything that hasn't been

29   cooked to the recommended temperature."

30 DAVID: I'd like to hear her tell that to Rocky Balboa.

31 ERIC: She would.

32 DAVID: *(Imitates Rocky.)* But I have a big fight tonight! I've gotta

33   down a dozen raw eggs!

34 ERIC: Oh, no you don't! Salmonella! Salmonella!

35 DAVID: *(Boxing into the air)* Salmonella won't touch me! Heck,

1   nothing touches me! Because I'm the greatest fighter in
2   the world! I'm Rocky Balboa! *(Continues to box into the air*
3   *with his fists as he hums the "Rocky" song.)*
4   ERIC: Good thing Rocky Balboa doesn't have my mom for his
5   mom. He'd have to stay home tonight.
6   DAVID: So what's it going to take? All the guys are going to the
7   skate park tonight.
8   ERIC: What's it going to take? Forty-eight dollars. You want to
9   give me a loan?
10   DAVID: I don't have any money! But you could always beg.
11   ERIC: Beg my mom to forgive me?
12   DAVID: No! Stand out on the street corner and beg for money.
13   You know, like the homeless people do.
14   ERIC: But I don't look homeless.
15   DAVID: Then mess up your hair, rip your shirt and throw a
16   little dirt on your face.
17   ERIC: You think it might work?
18   DAVID: It might.
19   ERIC: I guess it's worth a try. *(They exit as RACHEL and ALYSSA*
20   *enter.)*
21   RACHEL: My brother is such a loser.
22   ALYSSA: What did he do this time?
23   RACHEL: OK, you know that cookie dough we're selling for the
24   pep squad?
25   ALYSSA: Yes. I delivered the rest of my orders last night. What
26   happened? What did your brother do?
27   RACHEL: Eric sampled not one, but four, *four*, rolls of the
28   cookie dough!
29   ALYSSA: Oh no!
30   RACHEL: Cookie dough that had already been ordered and
31   paid for! All I had to do was deliver it last night.
32   ALYSSA: And it's not like you can deliver cookie dough that's
33   been partially eaten!
34   RACHEL: Oh, I was so mad!
35   ALYSSA: I bet!

1   RACHEL: And you know what his excuse to mom was? *(Imitates*
2   *ERIC.)* "I didn't know." Isn't that such a lame excuse? "I
3   didn't know!"
4   ALYSSA: What did your mom say?
5   RACHEL: That he's grounded until he comes up with the forty-
6   eight dollars to repay her for the cookie dough. *(Smiles.)*
7   Which will be like, forever.
8   ALYSSA: *(As they are walking off)* I thought you weren't
9   supposed to eat raw cookie dough.
10   RACHEL: I know! I heard it could make you sick. *(ERIC and*
11   *DAVID enter. ERIC has changed shirts and is now wearing a*
12   *ripped shirt. His hair is tousled, he has dirt on his face and*
13   *he carries a small can.)*
14   ERIC: Do you think I need a sign?
15   DAVID: Nah. I think your appearance says enough. Plus the fact
16   that you're standing on a street corner with a can.
17   ERIC: I guess.
18   DAVID: I'll step back over here so people won't think we're
19   together. *(He moves off to the side and opens a newspaper,*
20   *peeking over the top of it.)* Hey, you need to look more
21   pathetic!
22   ERIC: How do I do that?
23   DAVID: Try to look more miserable.
24   ERIC: I am miserable! *(After a moment, someone walks by and*
25   *drops a dollar into his bucket)* Hey, I got a dollar!
26   DAVID: See, it's working! *(A short pause, then another person*
27   *walks by and drops a coin into his can.)*
28   ERIC: *(Looking inside the can, then speaks to the person who has*
29   *just left)* A penny? Can't you do better than a penny?
30   DAVID: Forget him. Go back to looking downtrodden.
31   ERIC: Hey, I'm beginning to feel that way! *(Another person*
32   *walks by and drops a coin into his can)*
33   DAVID: How much?
34   ERIC: A quarter.
35   DAVID: Hey, little by little.

1   ERIC: Yeah, but at this rate, it's going to take all day.

2   DAVID: Maybe, but tonight you'll be at the skate park with me
3   and the guys.

4   ERIC: That's true. *(Another person walks by, but this time the*
5   *person stops and gives DAVID a strange look. After a*
6   *moment, he shakes his head and walks off, not leaving any*
7   *money.)*

8   DAVID: You win some, you lose some.

9   ERIC: Did you see the way he looked at me?

10 DAVID: I guess he's never been down and out on his luck
11   before.

12 ERIC: Or yelled at by my mom!

13 DAVID: Hey, someone's coming! Look sad! *(RACHEL and*
14   *ALYSSA enter.)*

15 RACHEL: So anyway, who in their right mind samples, not one,
16   but *four* rolls of cookie dough? I mean, he just ripped the
17   packages open, dug into them, probably with his grimy
18   fingers, and just left them there without even attempting
19   to hide what he'd done.

20 ALYSSA: Boys are disgusting.

21 RACHEL: My brother is disgusting. And it makes me wonder,
22   what's he going to do next?

23 ALYSSA: Don't hold your breath.

24 RACHEL: What?

25 ALYSSA: Your brother. *(Pointing)*

26 RACHEL: *(Seeing him)* Eric, what are you doing? *(ERIC attempts*
27   *to hide the can, but before he does, someone walks by and*
28   *drops a coin into it.)*

29 DAVID: *(Looking over the newspaper)* How much did you get?

30 RACHEL: What happened to you hair? And your shirt? Did you
31   rip your own shirt?

32 ALYSSA: You look bad!

33 DAVID: *(Coming to his rescue)* Hey, hey, back off! We're doing a
34   little experiment here?

35 ALYSSA: An experiment?

1   ERIC: That's right. It's a ... a ... school project.

2   RACHEL: A school project? Begging for money? This wouldn't

3   happen to have anything to do with eating raw cookie

4   dough, would it?

5   ERIC: Rachel, why don't you just walk on by and stay out of my

6   business!

7   RACHEL: Well, maybe I would if you would stay out of my

8   cookie dough!

9   ERIC: I didn't know that was your cookie dough! It didn't have

10   your name on it, did it?

11 RACHEL: Actually it wasn't my cookie dough; someone else had

12   paid for it!

13 ERIC: Well, I'm sorry! I'm so sorry for eating your precious

14   cookie dough! *(Another person walks by and drops money*

15   *into his can.)*

16 DAVID: Yes, we ... uh ... need to note that amount for our school

17   project. *(Anxiously)* How much did you get?

18 RACHEL: I'm telling mom!

19 ERIC: Stay out of my business, Rachel!

20 RACHEL: Then stay out of my cookie dough, Eric!

21 ERIC: Well, it's kinda too late for that, Rachel!

22 RACHEL: Then give me my forty-eight dollars back!

23 ERIC: You mean *mom's* forty-eight dollars!

24 RACHEL: Whatever!

25 DAVID: If you ladies will excuse us. *(Pulls ERIC aside.)* Let's go

26   find another street corner.

27 ERIC: Sounds good to me. *(They exit.)*

28 ALYSSA: Can you believe he was begging for money on a street

29   corner?

30 RACHEL: Oh, just wait until I tell mom!

31 ALYSSA: Maybe you shouldn't.

32 RACHEL: What?

33 ALYSSA: Well, he must feel pretty bad for what he did to stoop

34   down to begging on a street corner.

35 RACHEL: That's true.

1 ALYSSA: And he's probably embarrassed!

2 RACHEL: I didn't think about that. At least he's making an
3   effort to pay mom back.

4 ALYSSA: So let him try.

5 RACHEL: OK. I won't say anything.

6 ALYSSA: Come on, we don't want to be late for practice.
7   *(RACHEL and ALYSSA exit. ERIC and DAVID enter.)*

8 DAVID: This corner looks good. OK, stand right here. Now, look
9   sad. *(Messes his hair up a bit more.)* That's good.

10 ERIC: I do feel sad.

11 DAVID: Great! Feel the part! That'll bring in more money. OK,
12   I'll be right over here. *(Steps aside and opens his*
13   *newspaper.)*

14 ERIC: *(After a long pause)* No one is coming.

15 DAVID: They'll come.

16 ERIC: Would you have done it?

17 DAVID: What?

18 ERIC: Eat raw cookie dough?

19 DAVID: Heck yeah! I love raw cookie dough!

20 ERIC: I guess I'm just feeling guilty.

21 DAVID: Now you're feeling guilty?

22 ERIC: I didn't know it was my sister's stupid cookie dough
23   that'd already been paid for! I was hungry. I like cookie
24   dough.

25 DAVID: Who doesn't like cookie dough?

26 ERIC: And now ... now ... look at me! *(Begins to sniffle.)* I'm left
27   with begging on the street!

28 DAVID: Dude, you're being too hard on yourself.

29 ERIC: *(Begins to cry.)* It's just ... I really feel bad.

30 DAVID: Man, pull yourself together! *(Another person walks by,*
31   *stops, sees him crying and stuffs money into his can. DAVID*
32   *looks up as the person exits.)*

33 ERIC: *(Looking at the money)* Whoa!

34 DAVID: *(Rushes to ERIC.)* Whoa! You've got enough here to pay
35   for your cookie dough, including the tax!

1   **ERIC: Can you believe this?**

2   **DAVID: That crying stunt was what we needed!**

3   **ERIC: That wasn't a crying stunt.**

4   **DAVID: Stunt or not, you're going to the skate park tonight! Yes!**

5   *(Another person walks by and drops a coin into his can.)*

6   **ERIC: Come on, let's get out of here!**

7   **DAVID: Hey, you know what? You've got enough money to buy**

8   **us both some ice cream.**

9   **ERIC: Great idea!**

10 **DAVID: And I think I'll have some cookie dough ice cream!**

11 **ERIC: Not me! I'm staying away from cookie dough for a long**

12   **time!**

13 **DAVID:** *(As they are exiting)* **I wonder if you can get that Salmon**

14   **disease from cookie dough ice cream?**

15 **ERIC: Beats me.**

14. Kinsey Was Here

CAST: (1M, 4F) CARLA, KINSEY,
BRITTANY, ANGELA, SETH
SETTING: School hallway.

1 CARLA: Kinsey, where have you been? I thought you got sick
2   and went home!
3 KINSEY: No, I was scrubbing the stalls in the girls' bathroom.
4 CARLA: What? Why?
5 KINSEY? Apparently, I wrote my name in all the bathroom
6   stalls. "Kinsey was here."
7 CARLA: You did? Why?
8 KINSEY: Carla, I didn't!
9 CARLA: But you're the only Kinsey in this school!
10 KINSEY: So obviously someone else wrote it for me!
11 CARLA: Who would do that?
12 KINSEY: That's what I would like to know! Because I was
13   summoned into the office by Mrs. Hogg demanding to
14   know why I wrote my name in every stall with a little
15   heart around it.
16 CARLA: Did you tell her it wasn't you?
17 KINSEY: Yes, but Mrs. Hogg didn't believe me. She just
18   screamed and said if I didn't clean that graffiti off the
19   stalls, then I was headed to the alternative center.
20 CARLA: So what did you do?
21 KINSEY: I took the pink sponge and green cleaner that she
22   shoved in my face and I scrubbed the bathroom stalls. All
23   day! Scrubbing till my arm practically fell off!
24 CARLA: Kinsey, we need to find out who did this!
25 KINSEY: I'd love to, but how?
26 CARLA: Leave it to me, because I have connections.

1   KINSEY: What? You have connections? Carla, what connections
2   do you have that I don't have?
3   CARLA: Brittany Turner. And speaking of … *(Waves)* Brittany!
4   Hey, Brittany!
5   BRITTANY: *(Enters.)* Oh my gosh! Did you see what Seth did in
6   the cafeteria? It was so funny! He super glued four
7   quarters to the floor in front of the Coke machine and
8   everyone who walked by tried to pick them up! Lionel
9   even got a knife and tried to pry them up! And Jared just
10   wouldn't give up! He was kicking and stomping them! But
11   they're still stuck to the floor! Want to come see?
12   CARLA: Not right now, Brittany. I'm trying to do a little
13   detective work and I was hoping you could help.
14   BRITTANY: Sure. What's up?
15   CARLA: Brittany, would you happen to know who wrote
16   Kinsey's name all over the bathroom stalls?
17   BRITTANY: *(To KINSEY)* Oh, I saw that! That was cute! I liked
18   the little heart thing you drew around your name. Oh …
19   oh … and did you hear about Seth's plans to let loose a
20   hundred crickets in the halls tomorrow? He's hoping all
21   the chirping will drive the teachers nuts!
22   CARLA: Seth's a real prankster, isn't he? So back to Kinsey …
23   BRITTANY: And do you want to hear what he plans to do with
24   the granny panties?
25   CARLA: Not really.
26   KINSEY: Granny panties?
27   BRITTANY: OK, picture melted chocolate …
28   CARLA: Brittany, stop! What we want to hear is who wrote
29   Kinsey's name all over the bathroom stalls.
30   BRITTANY: *(To KINSEY)* You didn't do it?
31   KINSEY: No.
32   BRITTANY: Then isn't that plagiarism?
33   CARLA: No, it's called defacing school property!
34   KINSEY: Brittany, do you know who could have done this?
35   BRITTANY: *(Points.)* Ask her.

1   CARLA: Who's that?

2   BRITTANY: A new student.

3   KINSEY: Brittany, why would a new student write my name all

4   over the bathroom stalls?

5   BRITTANY: She might if her name was Kinsey.

6   CARLA: Her name is Kinsey?

7   BRITTANY: That's what I heard.

8   CARLA: Well, let's go find out! *(Pulls KINSEY over to ANGELA.*

9   *BRITTANY follows.)* **Hi.**

10 ANGELA: Hi.

11 CARLA: So we hear you're a new student to our school.

12 ANGELA: That's right. Yesterday was my first day.

13 CARLA: *(Offers hand.)* I'm Carla and you are?

14 ANGELA: Angela.

15 CARLA: *(To BRITTANY)* I thought you said her name was

16   Kinsey!

17 BRITTANY: Well, I thought ...

18 ANGELA: It is.

19 CARLA: But you just said it was Angela.

20 ANGELA: Angela Kinsey.

21 CARLA: Oh, really? Angela Kinsey, huh?

22 KINSEY: And what a coincidence. My name is Kinsey, too.

23 ANGELA: Your first name's Kinsey?

24 KINSEY: That's right.

25 ANGELA: Kinsey what?

26 KINSEY: Kinsey was here! Sound familiar?

27 ANGELA: What?

28 BRITTANY: Kennedy. Her last name is Kennedy.

29 ANGELA: Oh.

30 KINSEY: And let me tell you, I just love scrubbing walls!

31 ANGELA: You do?

32 KINSEY: Sure! *(Mimes.)* Shaking that green powder onto a

33   sponge, scrubbing the walls until my arm feels like it's

34   going to fall off. Definitely my idea of fun!

35 ANGELA: I don't really like to clean, but my mother does.

1 BRITTANY: Angela, I think she's being sarcastic.

2 ANGELA: Why?

3 KINSEY: Because you wrote my name ... or your name ... all over
4   the bathrooms stalls!

5 ANGELA: No, I didn't!

6 KINSEY: *Kinsey was here!* Oh, and for a little extra add on, you
7   drew a heart around it!

8 CARLA: So, look here, Miss Kinsey ... this new school of yours
9   doesn't allow any defacing of property!

10 BRITTANY: I should go get Seth. He needs to hear this speech.
11   Did you hear what he did in the gym last week?

12 KINSEY: And I realize you might have thought it was cute. A
13   nice little introduction of yourself to your new school, but
14   my name is Kinsey and I had to take the blame for what
15   you did! So you need to march yourself into the office
16   right now and tell Mrs. Hogg it was you and not me!

17 ANGELA: But ...

18 CARLA: And we don't mind being your personal escort.

19 BRITTANY: *(To ANGELA)* I'd run for it if I were you!

20 ANGELA: But I didn't do it!

21 CARLA: Yes, you did!

22 ANGELA: No, I didn't! I swear!

23 KINSEY: Carla, for some reason, I believe her.

24 CARLA: Yeah, me too. Then who?

25 BRITTANY: Seth?

26 CARLA: Brittany, I don't think Seth is going to sneak into the
27   girls' bathroom and write on the walls.

28 BRITTANY: He might. Last year he put petroleum jelly on all
29   the seats.

30 KINSEY: Yuck!

31 BRITTANY: *(Sings.)* "Slip sliding away!"

32 ANGELA: Who's Seth?

33 KINSEY: This prankster kid who's always getting into trouble.

34 ANGELA: Maybe he put someone up to it.

35 CARLA: That's a thought. *(Looking around the room)* And since

1   he's standing over there, I say we go and have a little talk
2   with Mr. Seth. *(They ALL walk across the stage to find SETH,*
3   *who is digging in his backpack.)*
4 SETH: Hey.
5 CARLA: Hey.
6 SETH: *(Stands.)* Hey, any of your parents work for a realtor?
7 BRITTANY: No, but my neighbor is one. Why?
8 SETH: I'm looking for a realtor sign.
9 ANGELA: There's one on the side of my house. We just moved
10   in. But I don't think you can have it. I think the realtor is
11   coming by for it next week.
12 SETH: Great! Can I borrow it?
13 ANGELA: I'm not sure.
14 SETH: *(Smiles.)* Because tonight, after it gets dark, I'm going to
15   post a realtor sign in front of the school. *For Sale!* That'll
16   be funny, won't it?
17 CARLA: Speaking of funny stuff ... Seth, when was the last time
18   you snuck into the girls' bathroom?
19 SETH: Who, me?
20 KINSEY: Do you see anyone else standing here who would have
21   to sneak into the girls' bathroom?
22 SETH: Seems like I did ...
23 KINSEY: Recently?
24 SETH: Let me think ...
25 ANGELA: *(Trying to be helpful)* Did you write something on the
26   stalls?
27 SETH: Didn't do that one!
28 CARLA: Heard of who might have done something like that
29   lately?
30 SETH: Oh, the Kinsey heart thing?
31 KINSEY: *Yes!*
32 CARLA: You know who did it?
33 BRITTANY: See! I knew he'd know!
34 SETH: And I'm no rat.
35 KINSEY: Well, you better become one really fast!

1   **CARLA: Come on, Seth!**

2   **SETH: Well, I heard ...**

3   **KINSEY: Yes?**

4   **SETH: That the person who wrote it ...**

5   **CARLA: Yes?**

6   **SETH: Wanted to remain anonymous.**

7   **KINSEY: Seth, you can't do that to me! I spent hours scrubbing**

8   **the stalls for something I didn't do!**

9   **BRITTANY: Then how about if you give Kinsey some clues.**

10 **ANGELA: Yeah! Like, was the person who wrote her name a**

11   **male or female?**

12 **SETH: Female.**

13 **CARLA: Color of hair?**

14 **SETH: Uh ... brown.**

15 **BRITTANY: Short or long hair?**

16 **SETH: Medium.**

17 **ANGELA: Straight or curly.**

18 **SETH: Straight.**

19 **CARLA: Is she tall or short?**

20 **SETH: Average.**

21 **BRITTANY: Thin or heavy?**

22 **SETH: Average.**

23 **ANGELA: Cute or ugly.**

24 **SETH: Average.**

25 **CARLA: Popular or a dork?**

26 **SETH: In between.**

27 **BRITTANY: In athletics?**

28 **SETH: No.**

29 **ANGELA: Band?**

30 **SETH: No.**

31 **CARLA: Choir?**

32 **SETH: No.**

33 **BRITTANY: Dance team?**

34 **SETH: No.**

35 **CARLA: Sounds like this girl has too much time on her hands if**

1   she's not involved in anything.
2   KINSEY: I have a question.
3   SETH: Fire away.
4   KINSEY: *What's her name, Seth?*
5   CARLA: Yeah, Seth! Tell her!
6   ANGELA: Come on, Seth!
7   BRITTANY: Yeah, come on, Seth!
8   SETH: Oh, the pressure! The pressure! OK, OK, OK, I'll tell you.
9   *(A pause as the girls stare at him.)*
10   KINSEY: Tell me!
11   SETH: Herminie McGillicutty. But you didn't hear it from me!
12   KINSEY: Herminie McGillicutty did it?
13   ANGELA: Who's that?
14   CARLA: That little ...
15   BRITTANY: That doesn't sound like something she would do.
16   SETH: Well, I heard ...
17   KINSEY: Yes?
18   CARLA: Tell us, Seth!
19   SETH: Well, I heard that Herminie McGillicutty wants to be
20   you. So she was, you know, doing a little play-acting.
21   *(Demonstrates writing.)* **Kinsey was here.** *(Mimes drawing a*
22   *heart.)* **As if she was you.**
23   KINSEY: She wants to be me? But why?
24   SETH: Face it, Kinsey, you've got what it takes.
25   BRITTANY: No, that's you, Seth.
26   KINSEY: I have what it takes?
27   SETH: *(Shrugs.)* So they say. *(He starts off.)*
28   BRITTANY: *(Follows him.)* Hey, Seth, I liked your quarter prank!
29   That was funny! What's the next prank you're planning?
30   Can I help?
31   KINSEY: Well, what do you know? I have what it takes.
32   CARLA: Come on, Miss Inflated Ego, let's go check out Seth's
33   latest prank. You want to come too, Angela?
34   ANGELA: Sure, thanks.
35   KINSEY: She wants to be me! Maybe everyone wants to be me!

1 **CARLA: I bet I can get those quarters off the floor.**

2 **KINSEY:** *(In her own little world)* **And why wouldn't everyone**

3   **want to be me?**

4 **ANGELA: What's your idea?**

5 **KINSEY: Because if I wasn't me, then I'd wish I could be me.**

6 **CARLA: I have some fingernail polish remover and maybe we**

7   **could drip it around the edges, and then pry it up.**

8 **ANGELA: Good idea.**

9 **KINSEY:** *(Steps away from the girls and throws her hands in the*

10   *air.)* **Kinsey was here!**

15. Free As a Bird

CAST: (1M, 1F) ANNA, CHRIS

1 ANNA: *(Alone, she rehearses what she will say to her boyfriend.)*
2 Chris, it's not you, it's me. *(Pause)* Chris, it's me, not you.
3 *(Pause)* Chris, I don't know how to tell you this, but ... it's
4 you ... I mean, it's me ... I mean, I feel like I can't breathe.
5 *(Gasps for air.)* Chris, don't hate me, but ... *(Quickly blurts it*
6 *out)* I want to break up! *(Takes a deep breath.)*
7 CHRIS: *(Enters, looking at his watch.)* I know, I know, I'm late.
8 Sorry.
9 ANNA: It's all right.
10 CHRIS: Me and the guys were shooting some baskets. I lost
11 track of time. Sorry.
12 ANNA: It's OK.
13 CHRIS: So, you wanted to talk?
14 ANNA: Yeah.
15 CHRIS: About?
16 ANNA: Well, I, uh ...
17 CHRIS: You said it was important. What's going on?
18 ANNA: Chris, this is hard for me.
19 CHRIS: What's wrong? Are you sick? Oh my gosh! Have you
20 been diagnosed with some fatal disease?
21 ANNA: No!
22 CHRIS: Then what? You said something major! Wait! I know!
23 You're moving! Your dad got transferred to another city!
24 But what does that mean for us? You think we can handle
25 a long-distance relationship?
26 ANNA: No!

1   **CHRIS: We can't? Are you sure?**

2   **ANNA: Chris, I'm not moving!**

3   **CHRIS: Oh.**

4   **ANNA: Gosh, you almost sound disappointed!**

5   **CHRIS: No, I was just trying to guess what this major ordeal**

6   **was.** *(Snaps fingers.)* **I know!**

7   **ANNA: I doubt it.**

8   **CHRIS: You want to break up!**

9   **ANNA: How did you know?**

10   **CHRIS: That's it?**

11   **ANNA: Well, I ...**

12   **CHRIS: You do?**

13   **ANNA: Well, I ... you see, I, uh ...**

14   **CHRIS: I can't believe this!**

15   **ANNA: But it's better than me dying or moving, isn't it?**

16   **CHRIS: No!**

17   **ANNA: No?**

18   **CHRIS: Well, if you died, well, gee, I could be happy knowing**

19   **you died loving me!**

20   **ANNA: You could be happy?**

21   **CHRIS: And if you were moving, well then I could find a way to**

22   **make this work. We could still talk on the phone, e-mail**

23   **each other ... But this ... this ... How could you do this to**

24   **me?**

25   **ANNA: I ... uh ... I feel like I can't breathe.**

26   **CHRIS: You can't breathe around me?**

27   **ANNA: I feel choked.**

28   **CHRIS: Choked?**

29   **ANNA: It's me.**

30   **CHRIS: You?**

31   **ANNA: It's not you, it's me.**

32   **CHRIS: You think I'm choking you?**

33   **ANNA: I don't think you're choking me! I just need space.**

34   **CHRIS: Space, huh?**

35   **ANNA: I guess I like my freedom.**

1   **CHRIS: Then that's what you're going to have!**

2   **ANNA: I'm sorry.**

3   **CHRIS:** *(Takes a deep breath.)* **You know what? This is strange,**

4   **but I suddenly feel like I can breathe again.**

5   **ANNA: Again?**

6   **CHRIS:** *(Smiles.)* **Yes!** *(Another deep breath)* **I forgot what it was**

7   **like to be free!** *(Stretches arms.)* **Free as a bird!**

8   ANNA: So I made you feel like you were caged up?

9   **CHRIS: I never thought so before, but just now when you broke**

10   **up with me and I realized I was free ...** *(Deep breath)*

11   **Ahhhh ...**

12   ANNA: You don't have to act so happy about it!

13   **CHRIS:** *(Gives her a hug.)* **Thank you, Anna.**

14   ANNA: You're thanking me?

15   **CHRIS: Thank you for realizing that we didn't belong together.**

16   ANNA: It was just this feeling I had ...

17   **CHRIS: You felt choked! And now I understand! Because now**

18   **I'm free!** *(Hollers.)* ***I'm Free!***

19   ANNA: *(Glares at him.)* So what are you planning to do with your

20   newfound freedom?

21   **CHRIS: Enjoy life once again!**

22   ANNA: What?

23   **CHRIS: No more late night conversations about icky feelings!**

24   **No more chick flicks at the movie theatre! No more**

25   **carrying books around that aren't even mine! And no**

26   **more worrying if I smell bad after shooting baskets with**

27   **the guys! Finally, I can be me! Free!**

28   ANNA: Sorry I drug you down, Chris!

29   **CHRIS: No, no, it's OK. It wasn't you, it was me! I'm not the kind**

30   **of guy who likes to be changed, and to be quite honest; you**

31   **were trying to change me.**

32   ANNA: I was not!

33   **CHRIS: No, it's OK. I'm not mad. It's just a girl thing. Change**

34   **the guy into what she wants. It's normal. But now ... now ...**

35   **I'm free!**

1   ANNA: Chris, stop acting so happy! I broke up with you!
2   Remember?
3   CHRIS: *(Takes her hand.)* And Anna, I appreciate you doing this.
4   ANNA: *(Snatches hand away.)* Stop it! Can't you cry or something?
5   CHRIS: *(Laughs.)* But I feel so happy! And so free! *(Moves around*
6   *the stage.)* I'm free! I'm free! I'm free!
7   ANNA: Stop it, Chris! Stop it!
8   CHRIS: *(Stops and looks at her.)* What?
9   ANNA: I've changed my mind.
10 CHRIS: About what?
11 ANNA: Breaking up.
12 CHRIS: You don't want to break up anymore?
13 ANNA: No. I take it back.
14 CHRIS: But you can't take it back!
15 ANNA: Yes, I can! I take it back! So, we're not broken up. I'm
16   still your girlfriend. Let's just say we had a little
17   misunderstanding.
18 CHRIS: But ...
19 ANNA: And tomorrow is our anniversary.
20 CHRIS: But ...
21 ANNA: Are you going to buy me something?
22 CHRIS: No.
23 ANNA: No?
24 CHRIS: Anna, I'm sorry, but I want to break up. I didn't realize
25   it until we had our little misunderstanding a few minutes
26   ago, but ...
27 ANNA: You want to break up?
28 CHRIS: Anna, it's not you, it's me.
29 ANNA: It's me?
30 CHRIS: It's me. For the first time in three weeks ... OK, almost
31   four weeks, I feel like I can breathe!
32 ANNA: Chris, you are such a jerk!
33 CHRIS: I don't mean to hurt you, Anna.
34 ANNA: Hurt? I'm not hurt! I'm happy! Can't you see that I'm
35   happy?

1   **CHRIS:** *(Looking at her)* **No.**

2   **ANNA:** *(Angrily)* **Well, I am! 'Cause now I'm free! Free! Free!**

3   *(Exits.)*

4   **CHRIS:** *(Takes a deep breath and smiles.)* **Free!**

16. Food Fight

CAST: (2M) RICKY, PAUL
PROPS: Pen, paper.

1 (RICKY and PAUL are sitting at a table doing homework,
2 reading, etc.)
3 **RICKY: What's another word for embarrassed?**
4 **PAUL: Humiliated.**
5 **RICKY:** (Writes.) **Thanks.** (After a moment) **What's another word**
6 **for beg?**
7 **PAUL: Uh ... I don't know. Grovel?**
8 **RICKY: That'll work. Thanks.** (Writes.)
9 **PAUL: What are you writing?**
10 **RICKY: A note to Jennifer.**
11 **PAUL: Next question. What did you do?**
12 **RICKY: Don't ask.**
13 **PAUL: Come on. I'm your best friend.**
14 **RICKY: What if you were at Ashley's house having dinner and**
15 **for some unknown reason, you turned into someone you**
16 **didn't recognize?**
17 **PAUL: I don't know what you mean.**
18 **RICKY: So last night, Jennifer and I were in the formal dining**
19 **room with her family, having a nice meal when this nice**
20 **guy that you see here turned into ... well, into a savage.**
21 **PAUL: What happened? What set you off?**
22 **RICKY: Jennifer's little sister, Lola. She was sitting across the**
23 **table from me. And every time I said anything, she rolled**
24 **her eyes or stuck out her tongue or kicked me under the**
25 **table.**
26 **PAUL: How old is she?**

1　RICKY: I don't know. Ten, I think.

2　PAUL: And you didn't ignore her?

3　RICKY: I tried!

4　PAUL: Go on.

5　RICKY: Then Jennifer's father wanted to know my opinion on

6　　　the standardized testing for students.

7　PAUL: Why?

8　RICKY: Because I'm against it, Paul!

9　PAUL: I didn't know that.

10　RICKY: Did you not listen to the speech I made to the student

11　　　council last week?

12　PAUL: Oh, that.

13　RICKY: So, trying to sound intelligent and impress her father, I

14　　　start in on the speech that I gave last week. "This country

15　　　is obsessed with tests!" *(Stands.)*

16　PAUL: Did you stand up at the dinner table?

17　RICKY: Yes I did because I wanted to make my point!

18　PAUL: Go on.

19　RICKY: As I continued, "Test scores only prove that some kids

20　　　are better at taking tests than others! I propose that we

21　　　take a good hard look on what these tests truly imply! Do

22　　　they evaluate character? No! Do they evaluate persistence

23　　　of an individual? No! And teachers spend weeks teaching

24　　　students to take tests rather than teaching something

25　　　more substantial!"

26　PAUL: Wow. I'm impressed! You sold me!

27　RICKY: So, I was all into my speech and I have everyone's

28　　　attention and do you know what Jennifer's little brat sister

29　　　did?

30　PAUL: I don't know. Rolled her eyes.

31　RICKY: Yes!

32　PAUL: So?

33　RICKY: So? *So?* I'm making an important speech and all she can

34　　　do is snicker and roll her eyes?

35　PAUL: You did say that she was only ten years old.

1   RICKY: And how rude was that?

2   PAUL: Sounds typical for a ten year old.

3   RICKY: Well, I was fuming!

4   PAUL: Uh-oh. What did you do?

5   RICKY: It was bad.

6   PAUL: Confession time.

7   RICKY: *(Still standing, he looks down.)* I looked down at my plate

8   and in some uncontrollable rage, I grabbed a handful of

9   mashed potatoes ...

10 PAUL: You didn't!

11 RICKY: And slung them in her face!

12 PAUL: Oh no!

13 RICKY: So you'd expect Miss Lola would start screaming, right?

14 PAUL: Well, yeah.

15 RICKY: But instead, she wiped the potatoes from her eyes,

16   looked up at me and smiled.

17 PAUL: That was nice of her. You know, not causing a scene or

18   anything.

19 RICKY: There's more. Besides the fact that Jennifer's

20   screaming at me and her father has jumped up and

21   looked as if he's about ready to strangle me. Then Lola,

22   with an evil, poltergeist smile, grabs a handful of

23   cranberry salad and torpedoes them my way!

24 PAUL: Oh no!

25 RICKY: Oh, but it gets worse! Then I'm throwing more potatoes,

26   her father's throwing ham at my head, Jennifer is

27   screaming, her mother is grabbing food before it gets

28   thrown! Food is flying! People are screaming. Except for

29   Lola. Oh, Miss Lola is laughing. Food is everywhere! On

30   the floor, the wall, the chandelier ...

31 PAUL: *(Laughs.)* This is a riot! *(Notices RICKY is upset.)* Oh, sorry.

32 RICKY: So, not only am I physically thrown out of the house,

33   but I'm also informed that I will never return to that

34   household again! As if it's all my fault!

35 PAUL: Well, you started it.

1   RICKY: I didn't start it! Miss Lola smarty-pants started it!

2   PAUL: I wish I could've been a fly on the wall.

3   RICKY: Well, if you had been, you would've been covered with
4   mashed potatoes.

5   PAUL: Cool! I mean, wow ... that's uh, sad. You know. So, you're
6   writing an apology letter?

7   RICKY: Yep. I'm trying.

8   PAUL: Have you talked to Jennifer since the, uh ... little
9   incident?

10 RICKY: Not in person or on the phone. But I received a nice
11   little text message from her last night. "I never want to see
12   you again!"

13 PAUL: Yikes. You really blew it this time.

14 RICKY: *(Back to his note)* How about "Spoiled rotten brat!"?

15 PAUL: I think you better leave that out, unless you're referring
16   to yourself.

17 RICKY: But she is! She just kept on and on and on!

18 PAUL: And you let her get to you.

19 RICKY: So what do I do now?

20 PAUL: Grovel. Beg. Crawl through broken glass.

21 RICKY: *(Thinking out loud, in an angry tone)* "Jennifer, blame
22   me for reacting to your sister's irritating, constant
23   harassment! And blame me for throwing a handful of
24   mashed potatoes in her face! Yes, blame me for
25   everything!"

26 PAUL: I don't think that's going to work.

27 RICKY: You're right, it's not.

28 PAUL: *(Thinking out loud)* "Jennifer, the reason I reacted the
29   way I did ..."

30 RICKY: Yes?

31 PAUL: Is because I forgot to take my medication."

32 RICKY: Liar.

33 PAUL: "Jennifer, I love you, but I can't stand your sister."

34 RICKY: That'll never work.

35 PAUL: "Jennifer, I love you, but I think this relationship has

1   come to an end."

2   RICKY: But she already broke up with you.

3   PAUL: I know, but I have to end this with a little dignity here,

4   OK?

5   RICKY: I guess.

6   PAUL: So that's what I'll do. I'll break up with her. *(Goes back to*

7   *note.)* I'll say we are incompatible. *(Writes.)* Hey, what's

8   another way I can say sorry? You know, sorry it didn't

9   work out.

10   RICKY: "I hate myself for hurting you, Jennifer."

11   PAUL: Oh, that's good. *(Writes.)* "And I hope we can remain

12   friends."

13   RICKY: I wouldn't count on it.

14   PAUL: *(Back to letter)* "Because sometimes people change and

15   must move on." *(Taps pen on paper.)* "And while I realize

16   my actions were juvenile ..." Hey, what's another word for

17   juvenile?

18   RICKY: I know!

19   PAUL: What?

20   RICKY: Food fight!

21   PAUL: Ah, shut up!

17. Barbie Girl

CAST: (2M, 3F) BRENDA, MARCIA,
CHRISTY, TONY, STAN

1   (At rise BRENDA, MARCIA, and CHRISTY are looking in the
2   same direction.)
3   BRENDA: I'd hate to be her.
4   MARCIA: Doesn't she just make you sick?
5   CHRISTY: (In a hateful tone, she sings.) "I'm a Barbie girl, in a
6   Barbie world!"
7   BRENDA: Does she act that way on purpose?
8   MARCIA: Guess she can't help the way she looks.
9   CHRISTY: Yeah. I'd take her looks, but not her personality.
10   BRENDA: I'd take her hair.
11   MARCIA: And her skin. Doesn't she look airbrushed?
12   CHRISTY: And her teeth are so perfectly straight.
13   BRENDA: And white. Sparkling.
14   MARCIA: She could do a toothpaste commercial.
15   CHRISTY: Do you think she ever eats?
16   BRENDA: I've seen her eat.
17   MARCIA: Doesn't that make you sick? People who can eat
18   anything they want and not gain a pound.
19   CHRISTY: Or get pimples.
20   BRENDA: She probably spends hours in the bathroom every
21   morning staring at herself.
22   MARCIA: I would.
23   CHRISTY: Yeah, me too.
24   BRENDA: (Flips hair) "Yes, I'm so cute!"
25   MARCIA: She could be a model.
26   CHRISTY: She's skinny enough.

1   BRENDA: *(Flips hair.)* "Don't hate me because I'm beautiful!"
2   MARCIA: She sure does laugh a lot.
3   CHRISTY: Why wouldn't she laugh? She's adorable and
4   everyone knows it.
5   BRENDA: Including her.
6   CHRISTY: All the boys think she's adorable.
7   MARCIA: My brother thinks she's hot.
8   BRENDA: Maybe we'd get half the attention she does if we acted
9   that way. *(Demonstrates by giggling, flipping hair, etc.)*
10   CHRISTY: Brenda, that doesn't look right.
11   BRENDA: *(Still giggling)* What? You don't think so?
12   MARCIA: I don't think you're doing it right.
13   BRENDA: Well, maybe I should figure out how to do it right!
14   CHRISTY: You really want to be like her?
15   BRENDA: Maybe for a day.
16   MARCIA: Or a week.
17   CHRISTY: Yeah. Or forever.
18   BRENDA: So instead of hating her, maybe we should imitate
19   her.
20   CHRISTY: Do you think?
21   BRENDA: Sure. We'll copy all her good qualities.
22   MARCIA: Does she have any bad ones?
23   BRENDA: Notice how she is always smiling? *(All three girls*
24   *smile.)* Wouldn't you rather hang around someone who is
25   happy?
26   CHRISTY: Good point.
27   BRENDA: So we should smile more.
28   CHRISTY: But what about the hair? I can't dye it blonde.
29   BRENDA: Forget the hair.
30   CHRISTY: But her hair is perfect. Long, shiny, bouncy ... My
31   hair never wants to cooperate.
32   MARCIA: What else? Besides smiling?
33   BRENDA: *(Staring)* Notice how she practically dances around
34   when she talks. It's like she puts so much into her
35   conversations. You can't help but be drawn to her.

1 CHRISTY: *(Smiling and moving around)* **Like this? Is this how it**
2 **should look? I'm smiling. I'm moving. Is this right?**
3 MARCIA: That's not right. In fact, that was bad.
4 BRENDA: You need to work on it.
5 CHRISTY: Then we all need to work on it! *(The GIRLS begin to*
6 *smile, giggle, and move around in a silly fashion.)*
7 BRENDA: I wonder what they're having for lunch today in the
8 cafeteria?
9 MARCIA: Oh, I hope it's not that nasty goulash.
10 CHRISTY: Let's hope that it's something good.
11 BRENDA: But what's good in the cafeteria?
12 MARCIA: That's a tough question to answer. "What's good in
13 the cafeteria?"
14 CHRISTY: Nothing!
15 BRENDA: Then maybe that's good.
16 CHRISTY: Good?
17 BRENDA: Yes! Because that way we won't eat.
18 MARCIA: And we lose weight!
19 CHRISTY: But I'm hungry!
20 MARCIA: But what would you rather do? Eat nasty goulash ...
21 *(Points)* Or look like her?
22 CHRISTY: Look. Tony and Stan are staring at us. Gosh, they're
23 cute!
24 BRENDA: Maybe it's working!
25 MARCIA: Yeah! We're doing just what she does! Smiling,
26 laughing, moving around in a cute way.
27 BRENDA: We're definitely getting their attention!
28 CHRISTY: Because we're cute!
29 MARCIA: That's right, we're cute!
30 BRENDA: So maybe we should thank her!
31 CHRISTY: *(Pointing)* Thank you Barbie Girl! *(Sings.)* "I'm a
32 Barbie girl, in a Barbie world!"
33 BRENDA: Hey, look! Tony and Stan are coming this way! Keep
34 smiling. *(THEY smile and giggle as TONY and STAN enter.)*
35 TONY: What's so funny?

1   STAN: Who are you laughing at?

2   TONY: Us?

3   STAN: Because we saw you staring at us and pointing our
4   direction.

5   MARCIA: No, we weren't pointing at you! *(Points.)* We were
6   pointing at her.

7   STAN: Scarlet?

8   BRENDA: That's right. Scarlet is our friend.

9   CHRISTY: That's right!

10 TONY: Scarlet hangs out with you three?

11 BRENDA: Yeah, sometimes.

12 TONY: When?

13 CHRISTY: When? We don't know. We just all hang out
14   sometimes, you know?

15 STAN: Where? At her house? You all go over to Scarlet's house?

16 MARCIA: To her house? Well, not there, but ...

17 BRENDA: We hang out with her at school.

18 TONY: Oh, really? Because I've never seen Scarlet hang out
19   with any of you.

20 BRENDA: Well, she does!

21 TONY: Yeah, right.

22 CHRISTY: Like in the halls! We say hi!

23 STAN: Wow.

24 BRENDA: And you two have deep and meaningful
25   conversations with her?

26 TONY: Sometimes.

27 STAN: Last week she asked to borrow a dollar from me.

28 CHRISTY: Wow! She must really like you!

29 TONY: Did you give it to her?

30 STAN: Of course I gave it to her! *(Looks her way, in a dreamy*
31   *tone.)* She's the most beautiful girl I've ever seen.

32 TONY: Breathtaking. *(All three GIRLS stare at her.)*

33 BRENDA: Flawless.

34 MARCIA: A magnet.

35 CHRISTY: Perfect.

1 **BRENDA: I'm jealous.**

2 **MARCIA: Me too.**

3 **CHRISTY: Ditto.** *(In a daze, they ALL stare at her. After a pause,*
4 *they ALL smile and wave, then look away, embarrassed.)*

5 **MARCIA: That was a friendly thing to do.**

6 **BRENDA: Yeah, nice to wave and not scream at her when she**
7 **realized we were all staring at her.**

8 **CHRISTY: I think she is nice. We should invite her over**
9 **sometime.**

10 **MARCIA: That's a good idea.**

11 **STAN: Hey, can I come, too?**

12 **TONY: Me too! Please?** *(The GIRLS shake their heads and start to*
13 *exit.)*

14 **MARCIA: Maybe if she came over this weekend she could give**
15 **us some pointers about doing our hair and makeup.**

16 **BRENDA: I bet she would!**

17 **CHRISTY:** *(Sings.)* **"I'm a Barbie girl, in a Barbie world!"** *(The*
18 *GIRLS exit.)*

18. Texas Size Zit

CAST: (2M) MIKE, CODY

1   *(At rise CODY enters with a Band-Aid on his face.)*

2   **MIKE:** Cody, what happened to you?

3   **CODY:** *(Mumbles.)* You know.

4   **MIKE:** What?

5   **CODY:** *(Mumbles.)* You know, just one of those things.

6   **MIKE:** What?

7   **CODY:** *(Mumbles.)* It's just one of those things, you know?

8   **MIKE:** *What?*

9   **CODY:** *I have a zit, OK?*

10 **MIKE:** And you're covering it up with a Band-Aid?

11 **CODY:** Yeah.

12 **MIKE:** Why?

13 **CODY:** Because!

14 **MIKE:** Because ... ?

15 **CODY:** Because it's huge, OK?

16 **MIKE:** Dang! How huge is it?

17 **CODY:** As big as they come! Believe me!

18 **MIKE:** Cody, chill out, everyone gets them. Even me. It's part of

19   being a teen. A fact of life.

20 **CODY:** Well, I don't want anyone seeing my huge fact of life!

21   Especially Amber!

22 **MIKE:** But Cody, don't you think Amber will notice that Band-

23   Aid on your face?

24 **CODY:** Yes, but it's better than her seeing my enormous zit!

25 **MIKE:** And how are you going to explain the Band-Aid?

26 **CODY:** Well ... I'll tell her that I got into a fight. Yeah, that's what

1   I'll say!

2   MIKE: Yeah, and then you'll have to keep lying when she asks,

3   "When? Where? Why? How? With who?"

4   CODY: That's true. I know! I'll say that I cut myself shaving!

5   MIKE: Cody, you don't shave. Do you?

6   CODY: Yeah. Well ... sometimes.

7   MIKE: If you want my opinion, I say you pull off that stupid

8   Band-Aid and face the world, flaws and all! Who cares

9   what Amber thinks?

10 CODY: Who cares? I do, Mike!

11 MIKE: Cody, if she can't handle a little pimple ...

12 CODY: Excuse me, but it's huge!

13 MIKE: Really, Cody, how huge can it be?

14 CODY: Man, it's the biggest thing I've ever had!

15 MIKE: And you don't think Amber's ever seen a zit before?

16 CODY: No, not like this one! And not on me!

17 MIKE: Cody, she'll still like you.

18 CODY: I wouldn't. Heck, I didn't even like myself this morning

19   when I looked into the mirror.

20 MIKE: Uh, question. Did you see yourself in the mirror with the

21   Band-Aid on your face?

22 CODY: Believe me, Mike, this looks better than the alternative.

23 MIKE: Why don't you take off the Band-Aid and let me see.

24 CODY: *(Quickly covers Band-Aid with hand.)* No!

25 MIKE: Then I can tell you if it really looks all that bad.

26 CODY: *(Still covering face)* No!

27 MIKE: Cody, you're acting like a girl!

28 CODY: No, I'm acting like a guy with a zit the size of Texas on

29   his face!

30 MIKE: Well, at least it's not permanent.

31 CODY: It feels like it is! And last night I tried everything to

32   make it go away. Lotions, creams, astringents, pure

33   alcohol ... Nothing worked! In fact, by this morning, it had

34   doubled in size!

35 MIKE: Dang!

1 CODY: And what if it keeps doing that? Doubling in size every
2   day? And before long, this zit takes over my entire face?
3 MIKE: Cody, I've never seen that happen to anyone before.
4 CODY: Because those people no longer show their faces in
5   public! They hide in their houses! In the dark! That's
6   probably why they started homeschooling kids!
7 MIKE: That's not true! But it would be cool if we could miss
8   school for having a bad zit day. And it wouldn't be like you
9   had to stay in bed because you have a fever and you feel
10   like crap. You can just hang out, play on the computer, and
11   watch TV until it disappears.
12 CODY: If it ever disappears!
13 MIKE: It will.
14 CODY: I hope and pray.
15 MIKE: And until then, you get to walk around looking stupid.
16 CODY: You think I look stupid?
17 MIKE: Cody, no one covers up a zit with a Band-Aid!
18 CODY: They would if they had this on their face! I'm telling you,
19   Mike, it's the size of Texas!
20 MIKE: At least it's not the whole U.S.
21 CODY: Yeah, and I hope the other forty-nine states don't pop up
22   tomorrow!
23 MIKE: *(As they exit)* If that happened, you'd really look weird!
24   Bandages all over your face. Hey, you'd look like a
25   mummy!

19. The Catwalk

CAST: (3F) ASHLEY, LAUREN, RAVEN

1   ASHLEY: Tell me, on a scale of one to ten ...
2   LAUREN: Why must I always rate everything for you?
3   ASHLEY: Because I like to hear your opinion. On a scale of one
4   to ten, how do I look?
5   LAUREN: Ashley, you know I have no sense of fashion. You even
6   told me that yesterday when I wore a blue shirt with black
7   pants.
8   ASHLEY: Forget that. Look at me and tell me what you think. On
9   a scale of one to ten ... One being blah and ten being hot ...
10   LAUREN: What is a five?
11   ASHLEY: What do you mean?
12   LAUREN: Well, if one is blah and ten is hot, what is five?
13   ASHLEY: I guess it's just OK. So is that what I am? Just OK?
14   LAUREN: No.
15   ASHLEY: Well?
16   LAUREN: Four.
17   ASHLEY: What?
18   LAUREN: Four. What would you call four? Just a little bit below
19   OK?
20   ASHLEY: I'm not a ten?
21   LAUREN: You asked for my opinion.
22   ASHLEY: But this is a new outfit! I thought you'd say I was a ten!
23   What's wrong with you, Lauren?
24   LAUREN: I told you I have no sense of fashion.
25   RAVEN: *(Enters.)* Hey! Are these new shoes not the cutest?
26   LAUREN: Wow! Those are definitely a ten!

1 RAVEN: Thank you. I've gotten at least a hundred compliments
2   on them today. Do you want to make that one hundred
3   and one compliments, Ashley?
4 ASHLEY: Sure. Cute. So, Raven, what do you think of my new
5   outfit?
6 RAVEN: That's new?
7 ASHLEY: *(Proudly)* Yes, it is.
8 LAUREN: Ashley wants you to rank her new outfit on a scale of
9   one to ten.
10 RAVEN: You do?
11 ASHLEY: Yes.
12 RAVEN: Do I have to?
13 LAUREN: One is for blah and ten is for hot.
14 RAVEN: Well, my shoes are a ten!
15 ASHLEY: And now me. What do you say, Raven?
16 RAVEN: *(To LAUREN)* Did you rate her?
17 LAUREN: Yes, but my opinion doesn't count.
18 RAVEN: Why not?
19 LAUREN: Because I have no sense of style.
20 RAVEN: Who told you that?
21 LAUREN: Ashley.
22 RAVEN: Ashley, why would you say that to Lauren? Didn't you
23   see how cute she looked yesterday? I loved that blue/black
24   combo you were wearing.
25 LAUREN: You did?
26 RAVEN: Yes! It's like the coolest new colors to wear together.
27 ASHLEY: Blue and black don't go together.
28 RAVEN: Maybe not in the past, but these days, it's hot.
29 LAUREN: I looked hot?
30 RAVEN: I'd say so.
31 ASHLEY: So ... back to me.
32 RAVEN: Back to you ...
33 ASHLEY: So, on a scale of one to ten ...
34 RAVEN: *(To LAUREN)* What did you give her?
35 ASHLEY: It doesn't matter what Lauren gave me. I want to hear

1   how you rank me.

2 RAVEN: And that's new? That ... uh ... thing that you're wearing.

3 ASHLEY: Yes! So?

4 RAVEN: Well ... *(LAUREN steps behind ASHLEY and holds up*

5   *four fingers, then points to herself.)*

6 ASHLEY: Is it really that hard?

7 RAVEN: It's not that hard. But what I like and what you like are

8   two different things. I mean, what I think is a one, you

9   think is a ten. You know what I mean?

10 ASHLEY: Are you saying that you would rate me as a one?

11 LAUREN: Ashley, a one is blah.

12 RAVEN: If I was honest ... I'm sorry, Ashley, I'd have to give you

13   a one.

14 ASHLEY: A one?! Lauren gave me a four!

15 LAUREN: A low four.

16 ASHLEY: Well, gee, thanks, Raven! Thanks, Lauren!

17 LAUREN: Don't be mad, Ashley.

18 ASHLEY: Well, how would you feel if you were just ranked a

19   one? Blah! Wait a minute! We haven't ranked Lauren yet!

20 LAUREN: But I didn't ask to be ranked.

21 ASHLEY: Well, if you rank others, you will also be ranked!

22 LAUREN: You make it sound like a law.

23 ASHLEY: It practically is.

24 LAUREN: But most of the time I don't pay attention to how I

25   look. I grab stuff off the hanger and throw it on. I'm not a

26   morning person so it's just not happening for me at that

27   hour.

28 ASHLEY: Let me see, on a scale of one to ten ...

29 RAVEN: I give her a ten!

30 LAUREN: You do?

31 ASHLEY: No you don't!

32 RAVEN: Yes, I do! I love the sloppy look! It's so in!

33 LAUREN: Thank you!

34 ASHLEY: I'm sorry, but I give you a one.

35 LAUREN: A one?

1 RAVEN: Don't listen to her.

2 LAUREN: Why not?

3 RAVEN: Because she's jealous.

4 ASHLEY: I'm not jealous of Lauren! Look at her!

5 RAVEN: Look at you!

6 LAUREN: Look at me? I don't look that bad, do I?

7 ASHLEY: Yes!

8 RAVEN: No!

9 LAUREN: Yes? No? What is it?

10 RAVEN: You look great, Lauren!

11 ASHLEY: She looks great for a Saturday morning with no plans
12   to see anyone.

13 LAUREN: Ashley! Just because I don't love what you're wearing
14   doesn't mean you have to be mean!

15 ASHLEY: I just thought we were all being honest here.

16 RAVEN: If we're all being honest here, then my shoes are a ten,
17   which makes me a ten!

18 LAUREN: And my sloppy look is a ten, so I'm a ten!

19 ASHLEY: And I think my new outfit is hot, so I'm a ten, too!

20   *(Pause as LAUREN and RAVEN stare at her)* Right? I'm a ten,
21   too? *(Pause)* OK, an eight? Or a seven? *(Pause)* Well, I'm not
22   a four! And I know I'm not a one! I'm not a one, right?
23   *(Pause)*

24 LAUREN: Maybe we should keep our opinions to ourselves.

25 RAVEN: Good idea, Lauren.

26 LAUREN: Because everyone has their own idea of what looks
27   good.

28 RAVEN: That's true.

29 LAUREN: So it's best to love what you love ...

30 RAVEN: And hate what you hate ...

31 LAUREN: And keep your opinion to yourself.

32 ASHLEY: So, Lauren, I shouldn't tell you that you look like you
33   just crawled out of bed?

34 LAUREN: *(To RAVEN)* Which is a good look, right?

35 RAVEN: It's hot!

1 ASHLEY: And Raven, I shouldn't tell you that your shoes are
2   hideous?
3 RAVEN: Hideously hot is how I'll take it. *(To Lauren)* **Aren't they**
4   **cute?**
5 LAUREN: I want a pair!
6 ASHLEY: And in *my* opinion, I could hit the catwalk!
7   *(Demonstrates as she swaggers in front of them in an*
8   *exaggerated fashion.)*
9 RAVEN: You're right!
10 LAUREN: She is?
11 RAVEN: Look at her! She's doing the catwalk!
12 LAUREN: That looks strange. And don't the models usually
13   wear, you know, cute stuff?
14 RAVEN: It's all about the attitude. Look at her!
15 LAUREN: That looks weird.
16 RAVEN: Ashley, you should do the catwalk all through the halls
17   today!
18 LAUREN: I wouldn't tell her that.
19 ASHLEY: I believe I will. *(Continues with her exaggerated moves*
20   *as she exits off the stage.)*
21 LAUREN: I'm never going to rate her again!
22 RAVEN: Back to my shoes. Aren't these the cutest?
23 LAUREN: They are cute.
24 RAVEN: Maybe we should do the catwalk, too!
25 LAUREN: As long as no one sees us! *(THEY swagger their hips as*
26   *they exit.)*

20. Save the Frogs!

CAST: (1M, 2F) KELSEY, CRYSTAL, DONNY
PROPS: Four boxes or trays, notepads, pens, trash can.
SETTING: Several small opened boxes or trays
are set out on tables.

1   *(At rise KELSEY, CRYSTAL, and DONNY are holding*
2   *notepads and pens. In a single file, they approach the first*
3   *box.)*
4 **KELSEY:** *(Looks inside the box, makes a face, then writes down an*
5   *answer. Turns to CRYSTAL.)* **I think it's a kidney.**
6 **CRYSTAL: Ewwww! I'll take your word for it. I'm not even**
7   **looking!** *(Writes in her notepad, then looks back at DONNY.)*
8   **Kelsey thinks it's a kidney.**
9 **DONNY:** *(Looks into the first box.)* **It's a liver.** *(Writes.)* **The liver**
10   **extracts impurities from the blood so they can be**
11   **eliminated from the body. It also converts food into**
12   **nutrients by creating bile, an important chemical that**
13   **digests food.**
14 **KELSEY and CRYSTAL: Oh!** *(Erases answers and makes changes.)*
15 **KELSEY: Let's move on.** *(Looks inside second box, makes a face,*
16   *then writes down answer. Turns to CRYSTAL.)* **I think it's a**
17   **spleen.**
18 **CRYSTAL: I trust you. I'm not looking.** *(Writes down answer,*
19   *then turns to DONNY.)* **Kelsey thinks it's a spleen.**
20   **Whatever that is.**
21 **DONNY:** *(Looks into the second box.)* **It's a kidney.** *(Writes.)* **The**
22   **kidney is brownish in color and located in the lower part**
23   **of the frog's abdomen.**
24 **KELSEY and CRYSTAL: Oh!** *(Erases answers and makes changes.)*
25 **CRYSTAL: Isn't this the stupidest science test ever?**

1   **KELSEY: Is stupidest a word?**

2   **CRYSTAL: I think so.**

3   **DONNY: It is.**

4   **KELSEY: Well, I agree, this is the stupidest science test! Naming**

5   **body parts! Please!**

6   **CRYSTAL: And disgusting!**

7   **KELSEY: Crystal, you haven't even looked in any of the boxes.**

8   **CRYSTAL: I have a weak stomach. And since Mr. Carter put us**

9   **in a group, I can rely on your expertise.**

10   **KELSEY: You mean rely on Donny's expertise. So far, I haven't**

11   **got one right.**

12   **CRYSTAL: That's OK, Kelsey. You tried.**

13   **KELSEY: Well, maybe I'll get the next one.** *(Looks inside the*

14   *third box, studies it for a moment, then writes down answer.*

15   *Turns to CRYSTAL.)* **I think it's a lung.**

16   **CRYSTAL: Sounds good to me.** *(Writes down answer, then turns*

17   *to DONNY.)* **Kelsey thinks it's a lung.**

18   **DONNY:** *(Looks inside the third box.)* **It's a stomach.** *(Writes.)* **The**

19   **stomach is a storage sac for food. It digests food by**

20   **breaking it into smaller particles.**

21   **CRYSTAL: Ewwww ...**

22   **DONNY: The enzymes and acids mix with the particles and ...**

23   **KELSEY: That's OK, Donny! Really!** *(Erases answer and makes*

24   *changes.)*

25   **CRYSTAL:** *(Erases answer and makes changes.)* **Thank you for**

26   **your wisdom, Donny. We couldn't have passed this stupid**

27   **test without you.**

28   **KELSEY: You know what this reminds me of?**

29   **CRYSTAL: What?**

30   **KELSEY: That game called Operation. Where you have all those**

31   **little body parts and you have to figure out what they are**

32   **and where they go.**

33   **CRYSTAL: Without getting buzzed!** *(Grabs Kelsey's arm.)* **Buzz!**

34   **You lose!**

35   **KELSEY:** *(Laughing)* **Seriously, have you ever heard of a science**

1 teacher giving a test like this? My brother always talked
2 about dissecting frogs, but he never did this!
3 CRYSTAL: Students, today our test is, "Guess the frog's body
4 parts!"
5 DONNY: Can we move on now?
6 KELSEY: Certainly. *(Looks inside the fourth box.)* Hey, I know
7 this one! It's a heart!
8 CRYSTAL: Ewwww! Not that I don't trust you, Kelsey, but I'm
9 going to wait to write down my answer. Just to make sure.
10 KELSEY: I don't blame you. Donny ... it's all yours.
11 DONNY: *(Looks inside the fourth box.)* You are correct. Just like
12 the human heart, the frog's heart has arteries and valves
13 that move blood from chambers and organs. Arteries
14 carry blood from the heart and the veins return the blood
15 back to the heart.
16 KELSEY: And we thank you for that little science lesson, Donny.
17 *(Writes.)* Box number four is a heart.
18 CRYSTAL: *(Writes.)* I think we're going to get a hundred.
19 KELSEY: I think so, too.
20 CRYSTAL: But I wonder ...
21 KELSEY: What?
22 CRYSTAL: I wonder where the rest of it is.
23 KELSEY: The rest of what?
24 CRYSTAL: The rest of the frog! The rest of the body parts! The
25 actual body!
26 KELSEY: Maybe the trash? *(The girls lean over and carefully look*
27 *inside a nearby trash can.)*
28 DONNY: Probably in the refrigerator.
29 CRYSTAL: Ewwww!
30 KELSEY: Do you think Mr. Carter is going to make us do that
31 operation thing tomorrow?
32 CRYSTAL: That'd be terrible! I couldn't put all the organs back
33 where they go!
34 KELSEY: Me neither!
35 DONNY: I could.

1   KRYSTAL: And thank goodness you're on our team, Donny!
2   DONNY: But knowing Mr. Carter, that would be an individual
3   test.
4   CRYSTAL: If Mr. Carter made me do that, I'd throw up!
5   DONNY: First, we'd slip on the surgical gloves ...
6   CRYSTAL: Count me out!
7   DONNY: Then pick up the silver tweezers, and carefully, one by
8   one ...
9   KELSEY: Without getting buzzed. *(Grabs CRYSTAL and makes a*
10   *buzzing sound.)*
11 DONNY: *(Mimes.)* Then, carefully, insert the kidneys back into
12   their rightful place.
13 CRYSTAL: Stop it! Seriously, I'm going to puke! *(Holding her*
14   *hand over her mouth.)* My frog would be covered with
15   vomit.
16 DONNY: Then the liver ...
17 CRYSTAL: Ewwww!
18 DONNY: The gall bladder, the stomach ...
19 KELSEY: Donny, we get the picture. Can this little lab
20   demonstration be over now?
21 CRYSTAL: *(Hand still over mouth.)* Please?
22 KELSEY: At least we should all get a hundred for this part of
23   our exam.
24 CRYSTAL: *(Hand still over mouth.)* Do you feel sorry for it?
25 KELSEY: For the frog?
26 DONNY: It's dead. It can't feel anything.
27 KELSEY: But it used to be alive, Donny. Just think, if Mr. Carter
28   hadn't killed it ...
29 CRYSTAL: It'd be basking in the sun on a lily pad right now.
30 DONNY: Mr. Carter didn't kill it.
31 KELSEY: Then who did? He had to cut it open to get its heart!
32 DONNY: They're already dead when they're sent to the school.
33 KELSEY: How do you know?
34 DONNY: I just know.
35 CRYSTAL: *(Hand still over mouth.)* How do they kill them?

1   DONNY: That I don't know.

2   CRYSTAL: Wow, there's actually something that you don't
3   know?

4   DONNY: But I do know that annually, three million frogs are
5   killed for the purpose of dissecting in the classroom.
6   However, there is now a new alternative.

7   KELSEY: What's that?

8   DONNY: Computer simulations.

9   CRYSTAL: I'd still throw up.

10 KELSEY: Mr. Carter needs to do that! Save the planet! Save the
11   animals! Save the frogs!

12 DONNY: Mr. Carter believes in hands-on experience.

13 KELSEY: How do you know?

14 DONNY: I heard him talking about it.

15 KELSEY: We should start a petition! Save the frogs!

16 DONNY: I disagree. Frogs are dumb. And we can learn from
17   them. *(Goes to one of the boxes and reaches inside.)* Take
18   this heart for instance.

19 CRYSTAL: What are you doing? Don't take it out!

20 DONNY: I just want to show you something.

21 KELSEY: Donny, you're not supposed to touch it!

22 DONNY: Just for a minute. I want to show you something! *(Lifts*
23   *out his closed fist and moves toward CRYSTAL.)*

24 CRYSTAL: *(Jumps back.)* Get away from me!

25 DONNY: *(Moves closer to her.)* If you'll look closely ...

26 CRYSTAL: No! I'm not looking at a dead frog's heart!

27 DONNY: But I want to show you something.

28 CRYSTAL: *(Covers her mouth.)* Do you want me to throw up on
29   your hand? Because that's what I'm going to do if you
30   show it to me!

31 KELSEY: Donny, don't.

32 DONNY: But look. *(Opens his hand.)* Look.

33 CRYSTAL: *(Removes hand from mouth.)* Where'd it go? Did you
34   drop it? *(Jumps back, looking on floor.)*

35 KELSEY: Not funny, Donny.

1 **CRYSTAL: You were just teasing me?**

2 **DONNY:** *(Begins laughing.)* **I thought that was funny!**

3 **KELSEY: Come on, Crystal. Let's go turn our papers in to Mr.**

4 **Carter. And I want to talk to him about my Save the Frog**

5 **campaign. I'm really serious about it, too!**

6 **CRYSTAL: I'll sign your petition if you start one up.**

7 **KELSEY: Thanks.** *(KELSEY and CRYSTAL exit. DONNY moves*

8 *over to one of the boxes and stares inside it for a long time.*

9 *He looks up, glances around the room, reaches into the box,*

10 *then lifts out his closed fist.)*

11 **DONNY:** *(As he exits quickly.)* **Cool!**

21. Hot vs. Cold

CAST: (2M, 1F) EDDIE, COLTON, STEPHANIE
PROPS: Notebook paper, washrag, bar of soap,
shower cap, two coffee cups.
SETTING: School classroom.

1 **EDDIE:** *(Stands at the front of the classroom, nervously holding*
2 *several pages of notebook paper.)* **My report is titled Hot**
3 **versus Cold. To assist me with my demonstrations will be**
4 **my friend, Colton Leatherwood.** *(Reads.)* **Hot versus Cold**
5 **by Eddie Schumann. The difference between the two is**
6 **astounding.**
7 **COLTON: Yes, quite astounding!**
8 **EDDIE: Colton, you aren't supposed to say anything yet.**
9 **COLTON: Oh. Sorry.**
10 **EDDIE:** *(Reads.)* **And how? How might you ask?**
11 **COLTON: The point, explained by Mr. Schumann.**
12 **EDDIE:** *(Gives Colton a look, then reads.)* **Take for instance, the**
13 **sun. The sun has a temperature of 6,000 degrees Celsius.**
14 **COLTON: Scorching hot! Burnt to a crisp!**
15 **EDDIE: But the coldest temperatures at Antarctica have been**
16 **recorded as negative eighty-nine point four degrees**
17 **Celsius.**
18 **COLTON: Freezing my butt off!**
19 **EDDIE: Colton!**
20 **COLTON: Sorry.**
21 **EDDIE: But my point today is to prove to you that neither hot**
22 **nor cold is superior to the other. But each has its own**
23 **unique features.**
24 **COLTON: As explained to you by Mr. Schumann.**
25 **EDDIE:** *(Gives Colton another look.)* **Take for instance, dirty**

1   clothes. *(Looks at report.)* **Hot water cleans grass stains,**

2   **grape juice, chocolate, ketchup, mustard, tea, and coffee**

3   **while cold water cleans baby food, jelly, toothpaste, and**

4   **soy sauce.**

5   **COLTON: Soy sauce?**

6   **EDDIE: I found it on the Internet.**

7   **COLTON: Oh.**

8   **EDDIE: So as you will see, neither hot nor cold is superior, but**

9   **each is needed for different circumstances.**

10 **COLTON: Soy sauce stains!**

11 **EDDIE: Colton, not yet!** *(Reading his report)* **My next example**

12   **would be regarding physical injuries. The question often**

13   **comes up as to which method is best in treating an injury.**

14 **COLTON: You want me to fall to the ground and sprain my**

15   **ankle now?**

16 **EDDIE: Sure.**

17 **COLTON:** *(Dramatically falls to the floor and grabs his leg.)* **Oh,**

18   **my ankle! My ankle! I've sprained it!**

19 **EDDIE: For sprains, a cold ice pack will reduce inflammation.**

20   **So in this case, cold is the best choice. However, in the case**

21   **of a sore muscle ...**

22 **COLTON:** *(Quickly stands, massaging arm.)* **Oh, man, I'm so**

23   **sore! Coach really worked us out hard yesterday!**

24 **EDDIE: In this instance, heat improves circulation and helps**

25   **minimize the pain. Another example I would like to offer ...**

26 **COLTON: Is this the shower example? Because I've got the**

27   **props right over here! Hold on!** *(Rushes to a plastic sack and*

28   *pulls out a bar of soap, washrag, and a shower cap. Puts the*

29   *shower cap on his head)* **Ready!**

30 **EDDIE: No, Colton! Next is the coffee example!**

31 **COLTON: Oh.** *(Puts the shower props aside.)* **Sorry.**

32 **EDDIE: Could you be a little quieter while I do this? Please?**

33 **COLTON: Oh, sorry. I was just trying to help. I guess I got a little**

34   **ahead of myself. Or actually ahead of you. So yes, I'll just**

35   **stand here and be quiet. See, I'm being quiet.**

1   **EDDIE:** *(Takes a deep breath and tries to compose himself.)* **Hot**
2   **coffee versus cold coffee. If we might have a volunteer**
3   **from the audience ...** *(Pause)* **Any volunteers?** *(Pause)*
4   **Anyone?**
5   **COLTON:** *(To the audience)* **Hey, Belinda, you'll do it, won't you?**
6   *(Pause)* **Why not? No it's not a stupid report!**
7   **EDDIE: I'll take care of this, Colton. So, if we could have one**
8   **volunteer. Any volunteers?** *(Pause)* **Please.**
9   **COLTON: Looks like you might be stuck with me.**
10   **EDDIE: Just one volunteer. Male or female.**
11   **COLTON:** *(Raises hand.)* **I volunteer!**
12   **EDDIE: Besides you, Colton.** *(To audience)* **Anyone?** *(Pause)*
13   **Stephanie? Myra? Chris? Jason?**
14   **COLTON: Come on, Stephanie!** *(Starts chanting.)* **Stephanie!**
15   **Stephanie! Stephanie!**
16   **STEPHANIE:** *(Gets up from her seat and joins EDDIE and*
17   *COLTON.)* **Fine! But you owe me for this, Eddie! So, what**
18   **do I have to do?**
19   **EDDIE: OK, we have two cups of coffee ... Give me the cups,**
20   **Colton.**
21   **COLTON:** *(Gets the two cups off a nearby table.)* **Here you go.**
22   **EDDIE: As you will see, Stephanie, we have two cups of coffee.**
23   **STEPHANIE:** *(Looks inside the cups.)* **That's not coffee! It's**
24   **water!**
25   **COLTON: Let's pretend it's coffee, OK?**
26   **STEPHANIE: Fine! It's coffee!**
27   **EDDIE: And my question for you, Stephanie ... Do you prefer**
28   **hot or cold coffee?**
29   **STEPHANIE: What do you mean, do I prefer hot or cold coffee?**
30   **Coffee is supposed to be hot!**
31   **EDDIE: On the contrary. Nowadays, you may choose between a**
32   **steaming cup of Joe or an iced latté. So as you see ...**
33   *(Holding out the cups)* **You have two choices. And neither is**
34   **right or wrong. Neither is superior. But both of these**
35   **beloved drinks are yours for the choosing.**

1 COLTON: Beloved drinks? Did you get that off the Internet, too?

2 STEPHANIE: I'd rather have a Coke!

3 EDDIE: But if you had to choose? A steaming cup of Joe, or an

4 iced latté?

5 STEPHANIE: I don't like coffee!

6 COLTON: But if you had to choose, Stephanie!

7 STEPHANIE: I told you, I don't like coffee!

8 EDDIE: OK. Well, thank you for your participation. You may sit

9 down now. *(STEPHANIE goes back to her seat.)*

10 COLTON: You can ask me.

11 EDDIE: Ask you what?

12 COLTON: Do I prefer hot or cold coffee?

13 EDDIE: Hot or cold coffee, Colton?

14 COLTON: Well, I have to agree with Stephanie. I'd rather have

15 a Coke.

16 EDDIE: *(Frustrated, he sets the cups down.)* Let's move on. My

17 next example ...

18 COLTON: *(Grabs the soap, washrag, and shower cap. Puts the*

19 *shower cap on his head.)* Ready!

20 EDDIE: It's not that one yet, Colton!

21 COLTON: Oh. *(Puts items away.)* Sorry. I'm just a step ahead of

22 you, aren't I?

23 EDDIE: If you would let me continue!

24 COLTON: Sure, sure. I know, I'm supposed to stand here and be

25 quiet. OK. Sorry. I'll be quiet now. You can continue. Go

26 ahead! What are you waiting for? Oh, me. OK, I'm zipping

27 my mouth. Sorry.

28 EDDIE: *(Frustrated, he looks at his report.)* My next example

29 would be hot drinks versus cold drinks for a hacking

30 cough.

31 COLTON: Isn't that like the hot and cold coffee example? Aren't

32 you repeating yourself here?

33 EDDIE: We're talking about a hacking cough.

34 COLTON: Oh yeah! That's my cue! *(Begins coughing profusely.)*

35 I'm sick! Sick! Sick! Sick!

1   EDDIE: Medically speaking, it makes no difference whether

2   you use hot or cold drinks as long as you continue to drink

3   fluids and prevent dehydration; eight-five percent of sore

4   throats are viral and will get better on their own.

5   COLTON: Dude, I know you got that from the Internet! *(Eddie*

6   *gives him a long stare, then begins coughing again.)* But I

7   don't have a sore throat! I have a cough!

8   EDDIE: However, cold drinks are shown to be soothing while

9   hot drinks help to release mucus.

10   COLTON: Mucus? Yuck!!

11   EDDIE: So again, I prove to you that neither hot nor cold is

12   superior to the other, but each has its own purpose.

13   COLTON: Uh, Eddie, aren't you supposed to take sides here?

14   EDDIE: What do you mean?

15   COLTON: Well, aren't you supposed to prove which is better?

16   EDDIE: I took that approach, Colton, but I couldn't find enough

17   evidence for either.

18   COLTON: But everyone else in the class is taking sides on their

19   issue. I picked mornings versus nights and night won.

20   Peter did sweet versus salty and salty won. Sid did male

21   versus female and ... well, we both know who won. So you

22   picked hot versus cold and you have to pick a side. You

23   can't be neutral.

24   EDDIE: Colton, this is *my* report, so I'll do it *my* way, OK?

25   COLTON: Fine. Don't blame me when you get one of these.

26   *(Makes a zero sign.)*

27   EDDIE: My last example ...

28   COLTON: *(Rushes to the props and returns with the washrag,*

29   *soap, and shower cap. He puts the shower cap on.)* Ready!

30   EDDIE: *(Rolls his eyes.)* Next time, remind me not to use an

31   assistant.

32   COLTON: Why? I'm adding to your point of view ... or rather,

33   lack of point of view.

34   EDDIE: My point of view, Colton, is that hot and cold are

35   equally important!

1 COLTON: And that's not what this assignment was about!

2 EDDIE: Would you just let me finish!

3 COLTON: My pleasure. Please, continue. *(Goes to the coffee cup*

4 *and pours water on the soap and washrag.)*

5 EDDIE: What are you doing?

6 COLTON: Getting ready for your next example.

7 EDDIE: You weren't supposed to do that!

8 COLTON: Are we not doing the shower example?

9 EDDIE: We are, but you are just supposed to stand there.

10 COLTON: Hey, I'm in drama and I like to act stuff out, OK?

11 EDDIE: OK, fine! *(Composes himself.)* My next example, hot

12 showers versus cold showers.

13 COLTON: I'm not saying a thing ... even though I don't see how

14 you can be neutral on this one.

15 EDDIE: Colton, will you shut up?

16 COLTON: Who wants to take a cold shower?

17 EDDIE: *(Ignores him.)* There is evidence to show that cold

18 showers in the morning prolong life.

19 COLTON: Well, you can't believe everything that you hear! I

20 don't believe it.

21 EDDIE: Especially when adding exercise and fish supplements.

22 COLTON: *(Laughs.)* Fish supplements?

23 EDDIE: *(Reading his report)* And cold showers also have the

24 following positive effects ...

25 COLTON: Brrrr! Talk about brutal!

26 EDDIE: *(Reading his report)* Increases circulation, contracts the

27 muscles to eliminate toxins, helps reduce migraines,

28 alleviates skin breakouts, improves metabolism, and

29 curbs the appetite. On the other hand ...

30 COLTON: On the other hand I'm sticking to hot showers!

31 EDDIE: Hot showers relieve stress, encourage a good night's

32 sleep, open pores ...

33 COLTON: Oh, oh, oh! I'm supposed to be doing something here!

34 *(Mimes taking a shower, singing loudly.)*

35 EDDIE: Colton, what are you doing?

1   COLTON: I'm taking a shower! Helping you with your report.

2   *(Continues with his shower and singing.)*

3   **EDDIE: Colton! Colton! *Colton!***

4   **COLTON:** *(Finally stops.)* ***What?***

5   **EDDIE: Why are you singing?**

6   COLTON: Because I sing in the shower, Eddie! Don't you?

7   Doesn't everyone?

8   **EDDIE: No, actually, I don't! And I didn't ask you to sing during**

9   **my report, did I? I just asked that you stand there next to**

10   **me and at the proper time, pull out the props and help to**

11   **demonstrate my point!**

12 COLTON: And I helped you demonstrate your point, didn't I?

13   OK, so maybe I wasn't quiet, but hey, I told you I was in

14   drama and you said that was great. In fact, you said that

15   was perfect.

16 **EDDIE:** *(Speaks slowly.)* **Just be quiet, OK?** *(Looks at his report.)*

17   **In conclusion ...**

18 COLTON: Aren't I supposed to do something here? You know,

19   for your conclusion?

20 **EDDIE: Forget it.**

21 COLTON: No! No! I don't want to forget it! I have a job here and

22   I'm going to do it to the best of my ability!

23 **EDDIE: I said forget it!**

24 COLTON: No! I don't want to forget it!

25 **EDDIE: Stop it, Colton! You're messing up this entire report!**

26 COLTON: Oh, is that what I'm doing? Messing up your report?

27   I thought I was here to add to it!

28 **EDDIE: Oh, you added to it all right!**

29 COLTON: I brought the props, I forced Stephanie up here, and

30   I demonstrated taking a shower. Wait. Was I taking a cold

31   or hot shower?

32 **EDDIE: It doesn't matter.**

33 COLTON: It matters to me.

34 **EDDIE: It was just a demonstration, Colton.**

35 COLTON: Which I totally messed up, right? You didn't like my

1   **singing in the shower and I'm sorry for trying to help!**

2   *(Takes off the shower cap and puts it on EDDIE.)* **Here, you**

3   **can do your own demonstrations from now on!** *(Exits.)*

4   **EDDIE:** *(After a pause, still wearing the shower cap, he looks*

5   *down at his report and reads dryly.)* **In conclusion, it is my**

6   **belief that neither hot nor cold is superior to the other,**

7   **but both are necessary in our day-to-day lives. And**

8   **sometimes it's just a matter of choice. Neither is wrong,**

9   **but both are important.** *(Looks up.)* **Thank you.** *(Forces a*

10   *smile, pulls the shower cap off his head, crumples up his*

11   *report, then exits.)*

22. The Worst of the Worst

CAST: (2M, 3F) JOHN, CARI, PAIGE,
MORGAN, MR. FREEMAN
PROPS: Detention slips, cell phone, snacks, stereo.
SETTING: Classroom.

1   *(At rise CARI is sitting at a desk working on an assignment.*
2   *JOHN bursts into the room. As JOHN and CARI talk, he*
3   *moves about the room.)*
4   **JOHN: Here I am! Detention! The room for rebellious teens!**
5   *(Looks around.)* **Where's the prison guard?**
6   **CARI: Stepped out.**
7   **JOHN: Perfect!** *(Stretches arms to the ceiling.)* **Time to make**
8   **plans for my escape.**
9   **CARI: You busting out?**
10   **JOHN: Only with my charm.**
11   **CARI: And has it ever worked before?**
12   **JOHN: First time, I begged for forgiveness. Second time, I cried.**
13   **Third time, I faked an illness. And this time, I'm putting**
14   **on the charm!**
15   **CARI: Well, good luck.**
16   **JOHN: Uncharted territory, but the expectations are high.**
17   **CARI: How many days did you get?**
18   **JOHN: The max. Three days. You?**
19   **CARI: Three. But this is my last.**
20   **JOHN: Would you believe I've only been at this school for three**
21   **weeks and it's already the fourth time in detention?**
22   **CARI: Shame on you.**
23   **JOHN: And you want to hear what my crime was this time?**

1 CARI: Sure. Why not?

2 JOHN: Well, being the artistic person that I am, I drew a picture
3   of a hamburger on the lunchroom wall. Graffiti, they
4   called it. And no, we're not talking about spray paint here.
5   But a simple pencil drawing of a juicy, mouth-watering
6   burger. And just when I'd finished this magnificent
7   design of a triple-decker burger, Mr. Freeman started
8   screaming at me. And I was like, "Hey, can't you let me
9   draw the French fries, too?"

10 CARI: You actually said that to Mr. Freeman?

11 JOHN: You bet I did! I thought the dull gray cafeteria walls
12   needed a little artwork! But unfortunately, Mr. Freeman
13   didn't agree. So, what'd you do?

14 CARI: *(Hesitant)* Well ...

15 JOHN: Come on, you can tell me!

16 CARI: Well, I work as an assistant in the school office ...

17 JOHN: Cool! Did you swipe some hall passes? Have any left?

18 CARI: No, I didn't do that. And I wouldn't do that!

19 JOHN: Oh. Then what did you do?

20 CARI: *(Takes a deep breath, then confesses.)* I was answering the
21   phone in an unprofessional manner.

22 JOHN: What do you mean? Like this? "Yeah, what do you want?"

23 CARI: No, not like that. But instead of saying *(insert school
24   name, if desired)* Lincoln Junior High, I said, "Burger
25   King".

26 JOHN: *(Laughs.)* Now that's funny!

27 CARI: And you wouldn't believe all the lunch orders I took!
28   Hold the mayo. Cut the onions. Super size that order ...

29 JOHN: *(Claps his hands together.)* That's great! You take burger
30   orders in the office and I draw burgers in the cafeteria!

31 CARI: Yeah, what a coincidence.

32 JOHN: So how many times have you been here?

33 CARI: This is my first time here and hopefully my last.

34 JOHN: No more prank calls, huh?

35 CARI: No. And no more office work, either. They're forcing me

1   **into the library. I get to help Mrs. Sneed shelve books.**

2 **JOHN: Exciting.**

3 **CARI: Yeah, right.** *(PAIGE enters, nervously looks around the*

4   *room, then quickly takes a seat.)*

5 **JOHN:** *(In a demanding tone)* **And what are you in here for?**

6 **PAIGE: Oh, are you the, uh ... teacher?**

7 **JOHN: Substitute teacher. They were short-handed today.**

8 **PAIGE: But you look ... well, never mind.**

9 **JOHN: Young?**

10 **PAIGE: Yes.**

11 **JOHN: You know, I get that all the time. You may call me Mr.**

12   **Johnson.**

13 **CARI:** *(Snickering)* **Mr. Johnson?**

14 **JOHN:** *(Slams his hand on a nearby desk.)* **And I'll have no**

15   **disrespect in this classroom!** *(CARI continues to smile at*

16   *him as PAIGE looks petrified.)* **This is detention, not**

17   **romper room!**

18 **PAIGE: Yes, sir.**

19 **CARI: Whatever.**

20 **JOHN:** *(Points to PAIGE.)* **You! What's your name?**

21 **PAIGE: Paige.**

22 **JOHN: May I see your detention slip?**

23 **PAIGE: Yes, sir.** *(Hands him a piece of paper.)*

24 **JOHN:** *(Reading it, he laughs out loud.)* **You squirted ketchup on**

25   **another student in the cafeteria?**

26 **PAIGE: It was an accident! I promise! Hilary was grabbing it**

27   **from me and I wasn't through using it and, well ... it just**

28   **squirted all over her face and in her hair. I didn't do it on**

29   **purpose! I promise!**

30 **JOHN:** *(Still laughing)* **Wish I could've seen that!**

31 **PAIGE: What?**

32 **CARI: Me too.**

33 **PAIGE: Mr. Freeman just assumed that I did it on purpose and**

34   **ordered me in here.**

35 **JOHN: I see.**

1 PAIGE: Is there anything you can do, Mr. Johnson?

2 JOHN: I'm afraid not, Paige. My job in here is to supervise, not

3   dismiss you for crimes you claim you didn't commit.

4   Because if I did that, well, we wouldn't have anyone in

5   here, would we? Because everyone claims he or she is

6   innocent, don't they?

7 PAIGE: But I am!

8 CARI: *(Raises hand.)* Me too!

9 JOHN: *(Points to CARI.)* Liar!

10 PAIGE: So I have to sit here for three days for something I didn't

11   do?

12 JOHN: Afraid so. Uh, just curious, but when you were in the

13   cafeteria, did you happen to see an artistic hamburger

14   drawing on the wall?

15 PAIGE: I saw part of a hamburger drawing. A janitor was

16   scrubbing it off the wall.

17 JOHN: No! No!

18 PAIGE: What's wrong?

19 JOHN: The janitor was ... uh ... scrubbing off the evidence.

20 PAIGE: Oh.

21 MORGAN: *(Enters, looks at JOHN.)* Is this detention?

22 JOHN: Yes it is. I'm the substitute teacher today.

23 MORGAN: You can't be! You look like a kid!

24 JOHN: Yes, I hear that all the time. Good genes, I guess.

25 MORGAN: How old are you?

26 JOHN: Give me your detention slip and sit down!

27 MORGAN: Sor-ry! *(Sits down.)*

28 JOHN: It's rude to ask an adult his or her age. Haven't your

29   parents taught you anything?

30 MORGAN: I'm sorry! *(To the other girls)* So what are ya'll in here

31   for?

32 JOHN: No talking, please! This is detention, not homeroom!

33   *(Looks at detention slip.)* What's this? You paid for your

34   lunch with pennies?

35 MORGAN: Yeah. So?

1 JOHN: *(Looking at the detention slip, he reads.)* **Held up the**
2   **lunch line while counting out 485 pennies.**
3 MORGAN: I needed to get rid of them, OK? Is that a crime?
4 PAIGE: Glad I wasn't standing behind you. Lunch is short
5   enough.
6 MORGAN: Two days of detention for paying with pennies. It's
7   not fair!
8 CARI: Doesn't sound like a crime to me.
9 MORGAN: And just when I had finished counting out my
10   pennies, there was Mr. Freeman.
11 JOHN: Ah, Mr. Freeman.
12 MORGAN: Do you know him?
13 JOHN: Do I know Mr. Freeman? Oh, yes. I know Mr. Freeman.
14   Very, very well.
15 CARI: And I have a feeling that after today you're going to know
16   him even better!
17 JOHN: Quiet now! Everyone be quiet!
18 MORGAN: So we just have to sit here all day?
19 JOHN: This is detention! What else do you expect, young lady?
20 CARI: Mr. Johnson, since you're just the sub ...
21 JOHN: Excuse me! Just the sub?
22 CARI: Who enters a new classroom every day and doesn't
23   receive the respect that he deserves ... And then has to get
24   stuck with us ...
25 JOHN: The worst of the worst!
26 CARI: And Mr. Johnson, we would like to make your job easier
27   today.
28 JOHN: And how would you possibly do that?
29 CARI: Well, if you would let us do whatever we want, then we'd
30   leave you alone. *(Smiles.)*
31 MORGAN: Sounds good to me.
32 PAIGE: Sounds good to me, too. Because I could like, totally use
33   a pedicure.
34 MORGAN: Yeah, and I've got a few phone calls I'd like to make.
35 CARI: And I have some dirt on someone in here that could get

1   him into a lot of trouble, if you know what I mean.

2 JOHN: Are you threatening me?

3 CARI: Me threaten you? I would never threaten a teacher! But I

4   will let the cat out of the bag if necessary.

5 JOHN: Fine! Everyone, do as you please! Phone calls, pedicures,

6   sneak out ... whatever!

7 PAIGE: Are you serious?

8 MORGAN: Cool!

9 JOHN: I didn't see a thing.

10 PAIGE: *(Takes off shoes.)* Thanks, Mr. Johnson!

11 MORGAN: *(Takes out phone and dials.)* Hey, Veronica, what's

12   up? Nothing, I'm just sitting in detention ... 'Cause some

13   psycho sub said I could ...

14 CARI: *(Takes out a snack and eats.)* Yum. I was hungry!

15 JOHN: *(Moves about the room as the others do their own thing.)*

16   Dang! This is so boring.

17 PAIGE: Mr. Johnson, you could sneak off to the teacher's

18   lounge? We won't tell.

19 JOHN: Uh, no. That's OK. I'll stay here and uh ... monitor this

20   classroom. Wish there was a stereo so I could play a little

21   music.

22 MORGAN: *(Points.)* In the corner, Mr. Johnson.

23 JOHN: What? Really? *(Finds a portable stereo.)* Yes! *(He tunes it to*

24   *a radio station and turns it up loudly. He dances about the*

25   *room as CARI eats, PAIGE props her feet on the desk, and*

26   *MORGAN talks on the phone. After a moment, the door*

27   *swings opens and MR. FREEMAN enters. Everyone freezes,*

28   *except for JOHN who hasn't seen MR. FREEMAN. CARI puts*

29   *away her snacks, PAIGE puts her feet down from the desk, and*

30   *MORGAN hangs up the phone. JOHN continues to dance*

31   *about the room. Angrily, MR. FREEMAN walks over to the*

32   *stereo and unplugs it. JOHN stops and suddenly realizes what*

33   *has happened.)* Mr. Freeman! We were just ... I mean, I was

34   just ... The sub left us alone and we were ... you know ...

35 MORGAN: I knew he wasn't the sub!

1   **PAIGE: You're not?**

2   **CARI: He's not.**

3   **MR. FREEMAN: Come with me, John!**

4   **JOHN: Uh-oh!**

5   **MR. FREEMAN: Class, as you will see, we have cameras**

6   **installed.** *(Points.)* **Right up there. Your substitute teacher**

7   **will be here in just a few minutes.** *(MR. FREEMAN and*

8   *JOHN exit.)*

9   **JOHN:** *(As he exits with MR. FREEMAN.)* **Look, if you'll let me**

10   **explain ...**

23. Hair Color

CAST: (1M, 3F) NICOLE, APRIL, BRANDI, PAUL
(NICOLE has dark hair, APRIL has blonde hair, and
BRANDI has any color of hair.)

1 NICOLE: *(Excited)* **Guess what I'm going to do?**
2 **APRIL: Tell Paul that you love him?**
3 **BRANDI: You are?**
4 **NICOLE: No! I'd die if Paul found out that I love him! It's**
5 **supposed to be a secret, remember?**
6 **BRANDI: Uh-oh.**
7 **NICOLE: What do you mean, "Uh-oh"?**
8 **APRIL: Brandi, did you tell Paul that Nicole is in love with him?**
9 **BRANDI: No!**
10 **NICOLE: Then why did you say, "Uh-oh"?**
11 **BRANDI: Because I might have mentioned it to Paul's sister's**
12 **boyfriend.**
13 NICOLE: You did? Why?
14 APRIL: Relax everyone. They broke up and they're not talking.
15 So Nicole, you're fine.
16 NICOLE: Unless he told Paul's sister before they broke up.
17 BRANDI: Nah. Sisters don't typically talk to their brothers so
18 I'm sure you're fine.
19 NICOLE: He better not find out!
20 APRIL: My lips are sealed. So, back to what you're going to do ...
21 NICOLE: Well, it's something that I've always wanted to do!
22 APRIL: Be a cheerleader?
23 BRANDI: Nicole, you aren't trying out again, are you?
24 APRIL: You are?
25 BRANDI: Why put yourself through that again?
26 APRIL: Nicole, remember last year how you cried for an entire

1   week? And every time Brandi and I thought we'd finally
2   gotten you past the tears, there you'd go again ... *(Imitates*
3   *her crying.)* And remember how you cried so hard that you
4   held your breath? *(Imitates her again.)* It was scary!
5 BRANDI: Nicole, don't try out! Please!
6 NICOLE: I wasn't going to! But wait a minute. Who says I'd lose
7   again?
8 APRIL: Maybe you wouldn't! Isn't there a saying, "third time's
9   a charm"?
10 BRANDI: This would be your third time to try out?
11 NICOLE: I'm not trying out again.
12 APRIL: She tried out in fifth grade ... if that counts.
13 NICOLE: Fifth grade doesn't count. That was in elementary!
14 APRIL: And they also say, "If at first you don't succeed, try, try
15   again."
16 NICOLE: I'm not trying out for cheerleader again!
17 BRANDI: Thank goodness!
18 APRIL: Then what are you going to do?
19 NICOLE: *(Takes a deep breath.)* OK, are you ready?
20 APRIL: Yes!
21 BRANDI: Tell us!
22 NICOLE: OK, OK. *(Short pause, then she smiles excitedly,*
23   *anticipating their response.)* I'm going to dye my hair
24   blonde!
25 APRIL: *(Gives her a strange look.)* You mean blonde streaks?
26 NICOLE: No.
27 BRANDI: You mean, all blonde?
28 NICOLE: Yes.
29 APRIL: Every strand on your head blonde?
30 NICOLE: Yes!
31 BRANDI: Why?
32 APRIL: Why?
33 NICOLE: Because blondes have more fun!
34 BRANDI: That's just another one of those dumb sayings. "Third
35   times a charm," "try, try again," "blondes have more fun."

1   It's not true, Nicole.

2   NICOLE: Yes, it is! Isn't that right, April?

3   APRIL: Well, yes, but ...

4   NICOLE: See!

5   BRANDI: You don't have more fun because you have blonde
6   hair!

7   NICOLE: Yes she does!

8   APRIL: Yes I do!

9   BRANDI: That's just a dumb saying!

10 APRIL: I don't think it's a dumb saying!

11 NICOLE: And it's true. April, how many guys have asked you
12   out this year?

13 APRIL: Hmmmm ... a lot. Maybe a hundred.

14 BRANDI: A hundred?

15 APRIL: Well, I said no to most of them! Seven of the guys I went
16   out with, four I broke up with, and one broke up with me.

17 BRANDI: That leaves two ...

18 APRIL: *(Smiles.)* I know.

19 BRANDI: You're a two-timer?

20 APRIL: They go to different schools!

21 NICOLE: See! Blonde hair! Lots of attention! And maybe Paul
22   will finally notice me!

23 BRANDI: Oh, he'll notice you all right!

24 NICOLE: So tonight I'm dyeing my hair blonde!

25 APRIL: But Nicole ...

26 BRANDI: Just an FYI ... they do make something called "Oops".

27 NICOLE: What?

28 APRIL: Oh, I've heard of that before. You better get some, just
29   in case.

30 NICOLE: Get what?

31 BRANDI: It's called, "Oops Hair Repair."

32 ARPIL: So if you dye your hair blonde, look in the mirror and
33   scream ... *(Screams, then smiles)* The Oops will fix it.

34 BRANDI: It might fix it.

35 APRIL: Might?

1 BRANDI: Probably. If you do it right away. But if you walk
2   around for a week with blonde hair and suddenly realize
3   you have no friends, it might be too late.
4 NICOLE: Have no friends?
5 BRANDI: Then you may have to go and see a professional. And
6   they can be very expensive.
7 APRIL: Maybe you should try wearing a blonde wig first to see
8   how it looks on you.
9 NICOLE: I'm not wearing a wig!
10 APRIL: I know! How about I put some of my hair near her face
11   and Brandi can see how you look as a blonde, OK?
12 BRANDI: That's a good idea.
13 NICOLE: No!
14 APRIL: Come on. Just try it. *(Moves her head next to NICOLE's*
15   *head.)* **OK, how does she look as a blonde?** *(Brushes as*
16   *much of her hair as she can onto NICOLE.)* **You'll have to tell**
17   me because I can't see.
18 BRANDI: Ewwww ...
19 NICOLE: *(Jumps back.)* **Don't go** *Ewwww ...* **! Because I know it**
20   would look good! And besides, you can't tell how it'd look
21   by pushing April's hair in my face!
22 BRANDI: Nicole, seriously, you look better with your dark hair.
23 APRIL: I agree.
24 NICOLE: But I want to stand out! I want people to notice me!
25   And I think my hair color is blah.
26 APRIL: Then go with streaks.
27 NICOLE: I want to go for something different. Not, "Oh, look,
28   Nicole got some streaks in her hair. That's nice." Instead,
29   I want, "Wow, look at Nicole!"
30 BRANDI: But there's a difference between "Wow, look at
31   Nicole!" and "Wow, look at Nicole!" *(Speaks one with*
32   *excitement and one with shock and disapproval.)*
33 NICOLE: I want to be noticed!
34 APRIL: But does it have to be your hair? How about some really
35   long fake fingernails or something like that? Something

1   not so drastic.

2 NICOLE: I know! What if I went half and half?

3 APRIL: What do you mean?

4 NICOLE: Half brunette, half blonde? That'd be cool, huh?

5 APRIL: No, I don't think ...

6 BRANDI: April, I don't think it matters what we say. She's

7   determined to do this.

8 NICOLE: That's right, I am determined to do this!

9 APRIL: But half and half?

10 BRANDI: *(Laughs.)* Sounds like a creamer.

11 NICOLE: That's not funny.

12 APRIL: Hey, there's Paul! Hey, Paul!

13 PAUL: *(Enters.)* Hey, what's up?

14 NICOLE: Hi, Paul.

15 PAUL: Hey.

16 APRIL: Paul, we were just talking and maybe you could offer

17   your opinion here.

18 PAUL: Sure.

19 NICOLE: April, don't.

20 APRIL: It's just for fun. Kind of like a "what if" scenario.

21 NICOLE: April!

22 BRANDI: So Paul, look at Nicole ...

23 NICOLE: Brandi!

24 PAUL: *(Looks at Nicole.)* OK.

25 BRANDI: And in your opinion, what color of hair should she

26   have? Her current color or go blonde?

27 APRIL: Or half and half?

28 PAUL: Half and half? Like the creamer?

29 APRIL: No. Like half blonde, half brunette.

30 PAUL: And I have to decide this?

31 NICOLE: Of course you don't! But it was great seeing you, Paul.

32 BRANDI: Paul, we respect your opinion.

33 APRIL: And Nicole really respects your opinion.

34 PAUL: Really?

35 NICOLE: Well, sure ...

1 PAUL: So, your natural color, blonde hair, or half and half?
2 APRIL: So, what do you think, Paul?
3 BRANDI: Because believe me, your opinion counts here! More
4   than you realize!
5 PAUL: Let me think ...
6 APRIL: Take your time. There's no hurry here.
7 PAUL: Can I choose something else? Or does it have to be those
8   choices?
9 BRANDI: Go ahead. Choose something else.
10 PAUL: I'm thinking ... Bright red streaks.
11 NICOLE: I love that idea!
12 APRIL: You do?
13 BRANDI: I like it, too.
14 PAUL: I think that would look good on you, Nicole.
15 NICOLE: Thanks, Paul!
16 PAUL: No problem. Well, see ya. *(He exits.)*
17 NICOLE: *(In a dreamy tone)* See ya ...
18 BRANDI: So out with the blonde and in with the red.
19 NICOLE: *(Still looking dreamy in the direction PAUL left)* Maybe
20   I should dye my eyebrows red, too ... and wear red lipstick
21   and maybe some red pants and a red shirt ... and ... and
22   maybe he will really notice me ...
23 APRIL: *(Hollers as she exits.)* Hey, Paul! Can we have another
24   opinion over here?

24. The Laughing Technique

CAST: (1M, 1F) TARA, RANDY
SETTING: Classroom.
PROPS: Straws, scissors.

1   (*At rise TARA sits at a desk cutting straws. RANDY walks by,*
2   *stops, and watches her.*)
3   RANDY: Why are you cutting straws?
4   TARA: They're for my anti-smoking project.
5   RANDY: You're using straws?
6   TARA: Well, I can't actually use cigarettes, can I?
7   RANDY: What about those candy cigarettes?
8   TARA: Randy, they don't make candy cigarettes anymore! Now
9   they're called candy sticks.
10 RANDY: Oh. Bummer.
11 TARA: Bummer?
12 RANDY: I don't mean bummer they don't make candy
13   cigarettes anymore, which might encourage kids to
14   smoke, but bummer you have to use straws, which don't
15   actually look like cigarettes.
16 TARA: Well, it's the best I can do.
17 RANDY: (*Picks up a straw.*) So, what are you going to do? Walk
18   around pretending to smoke, and then go into a violent
19   coughing episode? (*Coughs.*)
20 TARA: No! But I am looking for volunteers to perform a skit
21   that I wrote. And Mr. Wilson, my health teacher, said he's
22   going to pick the three best skits to be performed at the
23   elementary schools.
24 RANDY: Sorry, Tara, but I can't act.

1   TARA: Too bad, because you get to miss school for an entire day,

2   go eat pizza for lunch, and ...

3   RANDY: Miss school? Hey, you know what? I think I can act

4   after all! *(Dramatically)* **"Romeo, Romeo, wherefore art**

5   **thou Romeo?"**

6   TARA: *(Shaking her head)* That was bad.

7   RANDY: Oh. How about this! **"Give me Liberty or give me**

8   **Death! Smoke cigarettes and you die!"**

9   TARA: Uh, I'm the writer and you're the actor. You have to say

10   what I write.

11   RANDY: Sure, sure. *(Picks up a straw.)* But I might have a few

12   helpful add-ons.

13   TARA: I don't need help with the skit, Randy. I just need actors.

14   RANDY: And an actor you have! *(Smoking the straw)* Sure, kids,

15   you may think smoking looks cool as you strut around

16   with a straw ... I mean, cigarette ... But let me tell you what

17   this straw ... I mean, cigarette ... is really all about! *(Throws*

18   *straw on ground and stomps on it. Pointing at the audience)*

19   It will fry your lungs, that's what it will do! Smoking

20   causes cancer, cataracts, lung diseases, heart attacks,

21   asthma, and diminishes overall health! And studies have

22   shown that during the years of 1995 to 1999, smoking

23   caused 440,000 premature deaths! And that was annually!

24   So listen to me, you bratty kids, don't smoke, because it's

25   not cool! *(Tosses straw on the ground.)*

26   TARA: Wow.

27   RANDY: *(Proudly)* Good, huh?

28   TARA: I meant, wow, you really know your facts.

29   RANDY: Hey, I'm in health too.

30   TARA: Like I said, Randy, you have to follow my script. Not

31   make up your own.

32   RANDY: OK, OK. I was just giving you a little sample. And here's

33   something else you might want to add in that little skit of

34   yours! *(Picks up another straw and pretends to smoke.)*

35   **Cigarette smoke stinks!** *(Tosses straw to the ground and*

1   *waves arms in the air.)* **Yuck, yuck, yuck!** *(Picks up another*
2   *straw.)* **So don't smoke! Unless you want to smell like a**
3   **stinking ashtray!**
4   **TARA: That's not the approach I'm taking, Randy.**
5   **RANDY:** *(Picks up another straw.)* **And cigarette smoking**
6   **pollutes! It's one of the most common forms of pollution**
7   **on the planet! Jot this down, you miniature people! ETS!**
8   **Yes, that's right! ETS! Environmental Tobacco Smoke,**
9   **a.k.a.** *pollution!* **So, you want to go around polluting our**
10   **environment? Huh? Huh? Do you?** *(Tosses straw to the*
11   *ground.)*
12   **TARA: You're being a little harsh on the elementary kids, don't**
13   **you think?**
14   **RANDY: No! Sometimes you have to do a little screaming and**
15   **threatening to get your point across!**
16   **TARA: I was thinking I'd use the laughing technique.**
17   **RANDY: The laughing technique? What's that?**
18   **TARA: Where you get your point across using humorous**
19   **examples. You know, make the kids laugh.**
20   **RANDY: Tara, cigarette smoking is no laughing matter!**
21   **TARA: I know, but ...**
22   **RANDY:** *(Picks up another straw.)* **Back to our little ETS study.**
23   **TARA: You really did pay attention in health class, didn't you?**
24   **RANDY: If I might proceed ...** *(Picks up a second straw.)*
25   **TARA: Randy, this is my skit, remember?**
26   **RANDY:** *(Ignoring her)* **If smoking is so cool, then why don't**
27   **people walk around with one in each hand. Be double**
28   **cool?** *(Stands there and smokes from each straw.)* **See? See**
29   **how cool I am?**
30   **TARA: You look stupid!**
31   **RANDY: Of course I look stupid!** *(Tosses the straws to the*
32   *ground.)* **Or better yet ...** *(Picks up three straws and sticks*
33   *one in his mouth and attempts to talk with it there)* **Three!**
34   **One in each hand and smoking at the same time!** *(Looks at*
35   *TARA.)* **Don't I look cool?**

1   **TARA:** No.

2   **RANDY:** *(Tosses the straws to the ground.)* **Or if you want to look**

3   **really cool ...** *(Sticks two straws in his ears)* **You can try**

4   **smoking from your ears!**

5   **TARA: You look stupid, Randy.**

6   **RANDY: But why quit there?** *(Puts straws in his nose.)* **And then**

7   **you can stick one in your mouth and one in each hand ...**

8   *(Turns to TARA)* **And I look really cool, don't I?**

9   **TARA:** No.

10 **RANDY:** *(Strutting)* **And I can just strut around like this all day ...**

11 **TARA: Hope your hair doesn't catch on fire.**

12 **RANDY: Looking all bad ...**

13 **TARA: Bad is definitely the word.**

14 **RANDY: Spending all my money on ... Hey!**

15 **TARA: What?**

16 **RANDY:** *(Pulls the straws from his ears and nose and tosses them*

17   *on the ground.)* **That's another area you can cover.**

18 **TARA: What?**

19 **RANDY: While I was so focused on the health aspect and the**

20   **pollution, I didn't think about this!**

21 **TARA: What?**

22 **RANDY: The expense of cigarettes!**

23 **TARA: I've got that covered in my skit, Randy. In a humorous**

24   **way.**

25 **RANDY: Oh yeah? How's that?**

26 **TARA: Well, I have this homeless person begging on the streets**

27   **and ...**

28 **RANDY: A homeless person begging on the streets? That's**

29   **humorous?**

30 **TARA: You have to listen to the rest of it, Randy! Anyway, this**

31   **homeless person is begging for money so he can buy**

32   **cigarettes and this little old lady walks by and kicks him.**

33   **And then, as he's on the ground screaming in pain, she**

34   **yanks him up by his hair and whacks him a few times with**

35   **her newspaper. And then ...**

1   RANDY: And this is supposed to be humorous?

2   TARA: You didn't hear the rest of it, Randy!

3   RANDY: *(Staring at her)* OK.

4   TARA: OK, so the little old lady is whacking him across the
5   head like this. And then this superhero appears.

6   RANDY: A superhero? Superman?

7   TARA: Not Superman, just a superhero.

8   RANDY: Shouldn't your superhero have a name?

9   TARA: I'll think of a name, OK? So anyway, the little old lady is
10   whacking him across the head and the superhero
11   appears.

12 RANDY: The superhero with no name.

13 TARA: And the superhero pushes the old lady away ...

14 RANDY: The superhero pushes an old lady?

15 TARA: And then the superhero picks up the homeless man and
16   carries him to the moon ...

17 RANDY: Carries him to the moon?

18 TARA: Because there's no smoking on the moon! Duh!

19 RANDY: Who said?

20 TARA: Randy, it's just a known fact!

21 RANDY: Well, I mean, if the superhero gave the homeless man
22   a cigarette and he wanted to light up on the moon ...

23 TARA: With no oxygen?

24 RANDY: Well, that's a good point.

25 TARA: So anyway ...

26 RANDY: Back to the superhero whisking the homeless man to
27   the moon.

28 TARA: So, the superhero and the homeless man are on the
29   moon ...

30 RANDY: Does the homeless man have a name? Or is he
31   nameless, too?

32 TARA: He doesn't have to have a name for my skit.

33 RANDY: But the superhero should have a name.

34 TARA: I'll give the superhero a name, OK?

35 RANDY: OK.

1 TARA: So, anyway ...
2 RANDY: The superhero and the homeless man are on the moon
3   ... I'm still waiting for the comic relief here.
4 TARA: So the superhero tells the man he now owns the moon!
5   I mean, he now owns the entire planet!
6 RANDY: A planet he can't breathe on?
7 TARA: Randy, that's not the point!
8 RANDY: It will be the point if the homeless man dies. *(Grabs*
9   *throat.)* Air! Air! I can't breathe!
10 TARA: The point is ...
11 RANDY: Yes?
12 TARA: The point is ...
13 RANDY: The point is ... ?
14 TARA: The point is that there's no smoking on the moon! *(Pause*
15   *as RANDY stares at her.)* And he's not poor anymore! *(Pause)*
16   And the superhero saved the day!
17 RANDY: Uh, question. Where's the comic relief? You know, the
18   laughing technique you were talking about?
19 TARA: Randy, it's when the old lady was hitting the homeless
20   man with her newspaper!
21 RANDY: Oh. *(Pause)* That was funny?
22 TARA: Yes!
23 RANDY: Looks like you may need a little more help than you
24   realize, Tara. Can I see your anti-smoking script?
25 TARA: I'm still working on it. Actually, it's just in my head right
26   now, but I just need to write it all down.
27 RANDY: Well, why don't you leave the superhero part out and
28   try a different angle.
29 TARA: But I want to do comedy.
30 RANDY: *(Picks up straws.)* Well, you're off to a good start with
31   these. I know, why don't you not cut them in half and let
32   the characters walk around like this? *(Smoking a long*
33   *straw)* I look stupid, don't I?
34 TARA: Yes.
35 RANDY: *(To the audience)* So don't smoke, unless you want to

1   **look stupid!**

2   **TARA: I want to make sure the kids understand that smoking**

3   **makes you sick.**

4   **RANDY: Yes, I look stupid and** ... *(Falls to the ground, smoking*

5   *the straw.)* **I'm sick! I'm sick!** *(Coughing)*

6   **TARA: And if you smoke, you'll die.**

7   **RANDY:** *(Smoking and coughing)* **I'm dying! Dying!**

8   **TARA: Please.**

9   **RANDY: Dying! Dying! Dying!**

10   **TARA: Hurry up and die, will you?**

11   **RANDY:** *(Smoking and coughing as he lies on the ground)* **Dying!**

12   **Dying!**

13   **TARA: Will you die already?**

14   **RANDY: These cigarettes ... they ... they ... killed me!** *(Collapses.*

15   *A long pause as TARA continues cutting straws. He lifts his*

16   *head.)* **That was funny, wasn't it?**

17   **TARA: No.**

18   **RANDY: I thought it was.** *(Sits up.)*

25. Decision Time

CAST: (6F) HAILEY, OLIVIA, JORDAN,
ROCHELLE, VICTORIA, EMILY

1   *(At rise HAILEY, OLIVIA, and JORDAN are standing side by*
2   *side with their arms linked.)*
3   **HAILEY: OK, when Alex gets here, we're not letting him**
4   **through.**
5   **OLIVIA: Until he chooses.**
6   **HAILEY: One.**
7   **JORDAN: Not two.**
8   **OLIVIA: Not three.**
9   **HAILEY: But one. And when his decision is made, we all agree**
10   **to accept it.**
11 **JORDAN: Good or bad.**
12 **OLIVIA: Win or lose.**
13 **HAILEY: Boy or not.**
14 **OLIVIA: Gone are his flirting days.**
15 **JORDAN: Gone are the days of his so-called confusion.**
16 **HAILEY: Not knowing whom to pick.**
17 **OLIVIA: Because today we are making him choose.**
18 **JORDAN: Decision time is here!**
19 **HAILEY: Today, Alex, you pick one!**
20 **JORDAN: Not two.**
21 **OLIVIA: Not three.**
22 **HAILEY: But one!** *(Pointing)* **Hey, there he is!**
23 **JORDAN: What's he doing?**
24 **OLIVIA: Is that Rochelle?**
25 **JORDAN: I can't tell. I guess he's talking to her.**
26 **HAILEY: OK, he'll be here in a minute, so let's go through it**

1 **again.** *(The girls stand up straight, look ahead, and tighten*
2 *their arm link.)*
3 OLIVIA: Alex, we're not letting you through until you make
4 your decision once and for all.
5 JORDAN: And what decision, you ask?
6 HAILEY: Think about it, Alex.
7 OLIVIA: It's not hard to figure out.
8 JORDAN: Three girls who hate each other's guts ...
9 HAILEY: Standing in front of you today ...
10 OLIVIA: Bonded together ...
11 JORDAN: Who have put aside their differences ...
12 HAILEY: Their hatred for one another ...
13 OLIVIA: Their jealousies ...
14 JORDAN: To demand ...
15 HAILEY: Insist ...
16 OLIVIA: Force you to choose.
17 JORDAN: No more games, Alex.
18 HAILEY: No more split decisions, Alex.
19 OLIVIA: Or would that be triple decisions?
20 JORDAN: More accurate, but let's just stick with what we've got.
21 HAILEY: And no more Mr. Cool with three girlfriends, Alex.
22 Because today you pick one!
23 JORDAN: Not two.
24 OLIVIA: Not three.
25 ALL: But one.
26 HAILEY: *(Short pause)* I'd say we did that well.
27 OLIVIA: *(Suddenly)* Pick me, Alex!
28 HAILEY: Olivia!
29 JORDAN: No, pick me!
30 OLIVIA: Jordan!
31 HAILEY: Sorry girls, but he's going to pick me!
32 JORDAN: In your dreams!
33 OLIVIA: I'll win, hands down!
34 JORDAN: No, he'll pick me!
35 OLIVIA: No, me!

1 JORDAN: Me!

2 HAILEY: Stop it! Stop it!

3 JORDAN: Sorry.

4 OLIVIA: Yeah, me too. *(Looking in the distance)* Uh ... why is Alex

5   trying to hold Rochelle's hand? *(Pause as they stare straight*

6   *ahead.)*

7 JORDAN: Obviously she likes it because she sure is laughing.

8 HAILEY: I wonder what's so funny?

9 OLIVIA: She could push him away!

10 JORDAN: And why is she touching his hair?

11 HAILEY: And why is he still trying to hold her hand?

12 OLIVIA: *(After a pause)* Good, she got away.

13 JORDAN: Or he gave up.

14 HAILEY: Or they're meeting later. *(Calls out.)* Hey, Rochelle!

15   Rochelle! Over here!

16 OLIVIA: Hailey, what are you doing?

17 JORDAN: Why did you call her over here?

18 HAILEY: So we can find out what's going on.

19 ROCHELLE: *(Enters.)* Hey, what's up?

20 HAILEY: Hey, Rochelle! I just wanted to ask you something.

21 ROCHELLE: OK, sure.

22 HAILEY: Did you know that Alex is my boyfriend?

23 ROCHELLE: Excuse me?

24 OLIVIA: Well, actually, he's all of our boyfriends. *(The other*

25   *girls nod.)*

26 ROCHELLE: No he's not! Because Alex is my boyfriend! Two

27   weeks, going on three!

28 OLIVIA: Great!

29 JORDAN: You may want to join the three of us.

30 ROCHELLE: What are you talking about? And what is all this?

31 HAILEY: Rochelle, we're not lying. Alex doesn't know what an

32   exclusive relationship is.

33 ROCHELLE: What are you saying? I'm not his only girlfriend?

34 JORDAN: Alex and I have been going out since last year.

35 OLIVIA: And he's been my boyfriend for seven months.

1 HAILEY: Eight months and counting for me.

2 ROCHELLE: But I thought ...

3 HAILEY: We know. Believe me, we know!

4 JORDAN: That's why we all hate each other.

5 OLIVIA: Well we did, until we decided to combine forces.

6 ROCHELLE: What are you planning to do?

7 HAILEY: Well, everyday, Alex walks by here to class and we're

8 not going to let him through until he chooses.

9 ROCHELLE: Chooses? Chooses what?

10 HAILEY: One girlfriend.

11 JORDAN: Not two.

12 OLIVIA: And not three.

13 ROCHELLE: Then maybe I should join you, too! *(Links arms*

14 *with the girls.)* He either picks me, or ... or I'm out of here!

15 HAILEY: Our sentiments exactly.

16 ROCHELLE: And I thought Alex was crazy about me!

17 HAILEY: Same here.

18 OLIVIA: Me too.

19 JORDAN: Me three. Or is that four?

20 VICTORIA: *(Enters.)* Hey, what's going on? Why are you all, you

21 know, linked together?

22 ROCHELLE: Because, apparently, Alex doesn't understand the

23 word exclusive and he has four girlfriends!

24 VICTORIA: Alex has four girlfriends?

25 OLIVIA: That's right.

26 HAILEY: But today he chooses one, and only one!

27 JORDAN: Not two.

28 OLIVIA: Not three.

29 ROCHELLE: Not four!

30 HAILEY: But one! *(VICTORIA joins them, linking arms.)* Uh-oh.

31 You too?

32 VICTORIA: Since yesterday in history class!

33 HAILEY: Wow.

34 OLIVIA: Unbelievable.

35 JORDAN: Jerk.

1   ROCHELLE: It's getting worse by the minute.

2   HAILEY: But today he chooses. One, and only one!

3   JORDAN: Not two.

4   OLIVIA: Not three.

5   ROCHELLE: Not four.

6   VICTORIA: Not five.

7   ALL: But one!

8   VICTORIA: When do you think he'll be here?

9   HAILEY: Any minute now.

10   ROCHELLE: And won't he be surprised?

11   EMILY: *(Enters.)* What's this?

12   VICTORIA: Hey, Emily.

13   EMILY: What's with the linked arms?

14   JORDAN: It's Alex.

15   EMILY: Alex?

16   ROCHELLE: Let's just say that he needs to look up the word

17   exclusive in the dictionary.

18   EMILY: Why?

19   VICTORIA: Is five timing a word?

20   EMILY: Alex has five girlfriends?

21   JORDAN: Five that we know of.

22   HAILEY: I wonder if there's anymore?

23   EMILY: Is this a joke?

24   ROCHELLE: That's what I thought at first.

25   EMILY: I know this isn't April Fool's Day. *(Looks around.)*

26   Candid Camera?

27   OLIVIA: Why would we do that?

28   EMILY: Then it's true?

29   HAILEY: It's true. Believe us, it's true.

30   VICTORIA: And today we're making Alex choose.

31   ROCHELLE: One, and only one.

32   JORDAN: Not two.

33   OLIVIA: Not three.

34   ROCHELLE: Not four.

35   VICTORIA: Not five.

1   ALL: *(Except for EMILY)* **But one!**

2   EMILY: *(Links arms with the other girls.)* **And not six!**

3   HAILEY: Another one?

4   EMILY: Since Meg's birthday party last Saturday.

5   HAILEY: I thought he was grounded last Saturday!

6   JORDAN: I thought he had a family reunion!

7   OLIVIA: I thought his grandmother died!

8   ROCHELLE: I thought he was sick!

9   VICTORIA: I thought he was baby-sitting his little brother!

10 EMILY: He was with me. Sorry.

11 HAILEY: You know, there could be hundreds more out there.

12 JORDAN: Hundreds?

13 OLIVIA: Maybe every girl in school is going out with Alex.

14 ROCHELLE: Even Bertha Mae?

15 VICTORIA: And what about the other schools across town?

16 EMILY: That means there could be thousands!

17 HAILEY: And if he can lie to all of us ...

18 JORDAN: And to all of them ...

19 OLIVIA: Then he's scum!

20 ROCHELLE: So maybe we should make it easy for him!

21 VICTORIA: We make the decision, not Alex.

22 EMILY: In terms you can understand, Alex, "Take a hike!"

23 HAILEY: Here he comes.

24 JORDAN: I know. Whoever wants a cheater boyfriend stays. And

25   if you don't, you leave. *(Long pause)*

26 OLIVIA: OK, on the count of three ...

27 ROCHELLE: Whoever wants to keep Alex stays.

28 VICTORIA: And whoever wants to dump Alex leaves.

29 EMILY: Ready ...

30 ALL: One, two, three ... *(PAUSE as they stare ahead.)*

31 HAILEY: Did you see that?

32 JORDAN: Alex saw us standing here and took off running!

33 OLIVIA: Did you see his face?

34 ROCHELLE: He looked scared!

35 VICTORIA: Caught you, Alex!

1 EMILY: Bye, and don't come back!
2 HAILEY: Well, that's it. So much for Alex. We made the decision
3   for him.
4 JORDAN: I still think he would have picked me.
5 OLIVIA: No way! He would have picked me!
6 ROCHELLE: No, he would have picked me!
7 VICTORIA: I think he would have picked me.
8 EMILY: No, he would have picked me.
9 HAILEY: If Alex picked anyone, it was going to be me!
10 JORDAN: No way!
11 OLIVIA: You wish!
12 HAILEY: Well, he wouldn't have picked any of you!
13 EMILY: Yes he would have! I'm sure he would have picked me!
14 VICTORIA: And I'm sure he would have picked me!
15 ROCHELLE: No, he would have picked me!
16 OLIVIA: Then why don't we go ask him!
17 JORDAN: Yeah, let's go ask him!
18 HAILEY: Fine with me!
19 ALL: *(They run off screaming.)* "Alex! Alex! Wait up!"

26. Dreadful Dancing

CAST: (1M, 3F) TONY, MAXIE, BRANDY, SABRINA
SETTING: Outside the school building
at the end of the day.

1 MAXIE: So anyway, my mom agreed to let me get my nails done
2   for the Valentine Dance next Friday.
3 BRANDY: Who are you going with?
4 MAXIE: At this point, I'm wondering that myself.
5 BRANDY: Well, you can't go alone!
6 MAXIE: Oh, I could.
7 BRANDY: But would you?
8 MAXIE: Sure, if I wanted to stand by the refreshments.
9 BRANDY: So Chris is a definite no?
10 MAXIE: Chris can go jump in a lake!
11 BRANDY: Uh-oh. He asked Hailey to the dance, didn't he?
12 MAXIE: You know, I'd like to show up at the dance with the
13   hottest guy in town!
14 BRANDY: That'd be nice, but I'm afraid all the hot guys are
15   already taken.
16 MAXIE: This is just great! I finally get my mom to agree to let
17   me get my nails done and I get to go to the Valentine Dance
18   and talk to the punch bowl!
19 BRANDY: Maxie, there has to be someone you can go with.
20 MAXIE: You'd think.
21 BRANDY: *(Points.)* What about him?
22 MAXIE: Who's that?
23 BRANDY: I don't know, but let's go find out! *(Pulls MAXIE over*
24   *to TONY who is bouncing a ball.)* Hello.
25 TONY: Hello. *(Looks up at the girls.)* **Hello!**
26 BRANDY: So, my friend Maxie and I were wondering ...

1   MAXIE: Are you new around here? You don't look familiar.

2   TONY: Oh, I don't go to school here. I'm just waiting for my

3   friend, Josh.

4   BRANDY: Oh, so you go to school across town! The rich school!

5   TONY: Well, it's not exactly across town, it's...

6   BRANDY: *(Interrupting)* Which means you probably don't have

7   a date to the Valentine Dance.

8   TONY: What dance?

9   BRANDY: This is perfect, Maxie!

10   TONY: What's perfect?

11   MAXIE: Oh, silly me waited until the last minute to find a date

12   to the dance next week.

13   TONY: Hey, I volunteer!

14   MAXIE: You do?

15   TONY: Yeah! That'd be great! I've never been to a dance before.

16   BRANDY: Never?

17   TONY: This would be my first.

18   BRANDY: Uh ... what's your name?

19   TONY: Tony.

20   BRANDY: Tony, do you even know how to dance?

21   TONY: Everyone knows how to dance!

22   BRANDY: Prove it.

23   MAXIE: Brandy! He doesn't have to prove it!

24   TONY: You want me to prove that I can dance?

25   BRANDY: Yes.

26   MAXIE: Of course not. You don't have to prove it.

27   TONY: *(Begins dancing awkwardly.)* See, I can dance. Look, I'm

28   dancing. Like my moves? Check out my cool moves! *(He*

29   *continues to dance.)*

30   BRANDY: We'll be right back. *(Pulls MAXIE aside.)* Maxie, he

31   can't dance! Look at him!

32   MAXIE: Well, maybe we can teach him!

33   BRANDY: And you know what else? He's short!

34   MAXIE: Brandy, this whole thing was your idea!

35   BRANDY: I know, but from afar he looked taller and cuter! And

1   **look at him!**

2   **MAXIE: Well, I need a date!**

3   **BRANDY: Maxie, you're taller than him!**

4   **MAXIE: I'll wear flats!**

5   **BRANDY: And slump down?**

6   **MAXIE: Brandy, I don't care if he's shorter than me.**

7   **BRANDY: OK, fine!**

8   **MAXIE:** *(They return to TONY.)* **Hey, Tony, how about if we all get**
9   **together this weekend and practice some of those cool**
10   **moves for the dance next week? Brandy is an expert at**
11   **dance moves.**

12 **TONY: Are you asking me to the dance?**

13 **MAXIE: Do you want to go?**

14 **TONY: You bet! I'd love to go! My very first dance! Yea! I can't**
15 **wait!**

16 **BRANDY: Excuse us.** *(Pulls MAXIE aside.)* **Maxie, are you sure**
17 **about this?**

18 **MAXIE: Well, he is kind of cute.**

19 **BRANDY: But he's short!**

20 **MAXIE: He's available!**

21 **BRANDY: And a horrible dancer!**

22 **MAXIE: And we can teach him how to dance! You'll help me,**
23 **won't you?**

24 **BRANDY: How did I get myself into this?**

25 **MAXIE: Brandy! Please!**

26 **BRANDY: Of course I'll help you!**

27 **MAXIE: Come on.** *(They return to TONY.)*

28 **TONY: Hey, I know! Last week I saw this old movie with John**
29 **Travolta called *Saturday Night Fever*. I could dance like**
30 **him!** *(Imitates the John Travolta move as he moves his hand*
31 *from the ceiling to the floor.)* **Want me to do this?**

32 **BRANDY: No! Please, no!**

33 **TONY: And Maxie, you and I could take over the dance floor!**
34 **Then I could stand in the center and do this!** *(Continues*
35 *with the moves, singing.)* **"Fever, night, fever, night, fever ... "**

1   MAXIE: Uh, Tony, I don't think you should do that!

2   TONY: Have you ever seen that movie? John Travolta was cool!

3   BRANDY: Tony, that was like fifty years ago!

4   TONY: It wasn't that long ago. Or wait, wait! I know!

5   MAXIE: What?

6   TONY: Have you ever seen that movie "Dirty Dancing"?

7   BRANDY: Forget it, Tony.

8   TONY: No, no, listen! I could stand at the front near the band or

9   D.J., then you could run through the crowd and I could

10   catch you and lift you up in the air! Like this! Want to

11   practice?

12 BRANDY: No!

13 MAXIE: No, Tony!

14 TONY: And if you can wear a full skirt, I can flip it up while you

15   turn in circles!

16 BRANDY: No!

17 MAXIE: No!

18 TONY: It was just an idea! I thought it would be cool. Plus, we'd

19   be like the main attraction at the dance!

20 MAXIE: I'd rather just have a date to the dance and mingle and

21   blend. You know?

22 TONY: Or we could go rent these matching outfits ...

23 BRANDY and MAXIE: *No!*

24 TONY: Strut across the dance floor like we owned it ...

25 BRANDY and MAXIE: *No!*

26 TONY: I'll hold your hand and twirl you out onto the floor like

27   this ... *(Demonstrates.)*

28 BRANDY and MAXIE: *No!*

29 TONY: And then you squat down and I raise my leg over your

30   head like this ... *(Demonstrates.)*

31 BRANDY and MAXIE: *No!*

32 TONY: And then I'll go down into the splits. *(Attempts to do the*

33   *splits.)* OK, OK, maybe not that. Wow, that hurt!

34 BRANDY: No one dances like that, Tony!

35 TONY: They don't? On TV they do.

1 MAXIE: Tony, you've never been to a dance and we're telling
2   you, they don't dance like that!
3 TONY: But we could stand out from the rest of the crowd! Like
4   Johnny and Baby did in "Dirty Dancing"!
5 BRANDY and MAXIE: *No!*
6 TONY: Or ...
7 BRANDY and MAXIE: *No!*
8 TONY: OK, OK. I guess I can just learn the latest moves at your
9   house this weekend.
10 MAXIE: Thank you.
11 TONY: But if you change your mind, call me and I'll bring over
12   those DVDs so we can watch them and copy their moves.
13 MAXIE: Sure, but I wouldn't count on it.
14 TONY: And in the meantime, I will practice my dancing!
15   *(Dances.)*
16 BRANDY: Excuse us for a minute. *(Pulls MAXIE aside.)*
17 TONY: No problem.
18 BRANDY: Maxie, there's still time for you to get out of this!
19   *(Pointing)* Look at him!
20 MAXIE: Brandy, I don't want to go to the dance alone!
21   Especially with Chris taking Hailey!
22 BRANDY: But do you want Chris laughing at you for going with
23   ... with *that?*
24 MAXIE: And we're going to teach him how to dance this
25   weekend, remember? And if worse comes to worse and
26   he's still dreadful, we'll just dance the slow songs. Surely
27   he can't mess that up!
28 TONY: Hey, Maxie, I'm going to buy you a corsage to wear on
29   your dress, OK?
30 MAXIE: I'm not wearing a dress!
31 TONY: And you can get me one of those boutonniere thingies.
32 BRANDY: Tony, this isn't the prom! It's just a Valentine Dance.
33 MAXIE: I'm wearing jeans.
34 TONY: Jeans?
35 MAXIE: Yes!

1 TONY: And you don't want one of those flowers to put right
2   here? Or one for your wrist?
3 MAXIE: No!
4 TONY: So I shouldn't rent that tuxedo?
5 BRANDY: Look, Tony, maybe for the prom...
6 TONY: Gosh, that'll be in like five or six years!
7 MAXIE: Five or six years?
8 BRANDY: Don't you mean in two or three years?
9 TONY: *(Counting on his fingers)* No. About five more years till
10   the prom for me ... that is assuming I go my junior year.
11 BRANDY: Oh my gosh! What grade are you in?
12 TONY: Does it matter?
13 BRANDY: It might!
14 MAXIE: Tony, you don't go to school across town, do you?
15 TONY: I never said I went to school across town.
16 BRANDY: Then where do you go to school?
17 TONY: Well, you know ...
18 BRANDY: No, we don't know! Tell us!
19 TONY: Just down the street.
20 BRANDY: At Travis Elementary?
21 TONY: Yeah.
22 MAXIE: *Travis Elementary?*
23 BRANDY: *Travis Elementary?*
24 TONY: Yeah, so?
25 BRANDY: *You're a sixth grader?*
26 MAXIE: Oh my gosh! I can't believe I have a date to the
27   Valentine Dance with a sixth grader!
28 BRANDY: I told you he was short!
29 MAXIE: I thought he was just short for his age!
30 BRANDY: He is short for his age!
31 TONY: Hey, I can still go to the dance. Dance lessons this
32   weekend, right?
33 BRANDY and MAXIE: No!
34 TONY: No?
35 MAXIE: I ... I ... I have to ...

1   **BRANDY: She has to wash her hair! Sorry!** *(Pulls MAXIE away as*
2   *they run off.)*
3   **TONY: But ... OK. See ya.** *(Continues with his dance moves.)*

27. Free Advice

CAST: (2M, 3F) ZACH, MADISON, CARLY, REBECCA, JOEY
SETTING: School cafeteria.
PROPS: Table, two chairs, tissues.

1   *(At rise MADISON is sitting at a table in the cafeteria. A sign*
2   *taped to the table reads: 'Free Advice'. ZACH enters.)*
3   **ZACH: What's this? Free advice?**
4   **MADISON: That's right. May I help you?**
5   **ZACH:** *(Looks around the room.)* **Uh ... this is the cafeteria.**
6   **MADISON: I know.**
7   **ZACH:** *(As if she doesn't know)* **Where you eat lunch.**
8   **MADISON: And have the opportunity to speak to a counselor at**
9   **the same time.**
10 **ZACH: Do the teachers know you're doing this?**
11 **MADISON: Mrs. Harris and Mrs. Rodriguez have both walked**
12   **by and smiled at me so I guess it's OK.**
13 **ZACH: And you're doing this for free?**
14 **MADISON: You read the sign. Free advice.**
15 **ZACH: OK, Miss Smarty Pants, I'll try out your free advice.**
16 **MADISON:** *(Sits up straight.)* **All right. How may I help you?**
17 **ZACH: Well, I can't decide. Do I eat the Salisbury steak or the**
18   **chicken nuggets?**
19 **MADISON: That's not the type of advice I give.**
20 **ZACH: Why not?**
21 **MADISON: My advice is on more important issues.**
22 **ZACH: Such as?**
23 **MADISON: Such as boyfriend or girlfriend problems. Issues at**
24   **home. Dealing with the death of a loved one.**
25 **ZACH: So you can give me advice for dealing with my pet's**
26   **death, but not figuring out what to eat?**

1 MADISON: My advice ... listen to your instincts.

2 ZACH: My instincts, huh? Well, half of my instincts are saying
3   the Salisbury steak is gross and other half of my instincts
4   is saying the chicken nuggets are a sorry excuse for
5   feeding a growing teen. So you tell me, Miss Free Advice
6   Person, what am I to do?

7 MADISON: Go with the Salisbury steak.

8 ZACH: The Salisbury steak? Why?

9 MADISON: It looks good.

10 ZACH: But I hate the Salisbury steak!

11 MADISON: Then go with the chicken nuggets.

12 ZACH: The chicken nuggets? Have you ever tried their chicken
13   nuggets? They taste like rock nuggets!

14 MADISON: Then dip them in ketchup.

15 ZACH: But who wants to eat a rock hard chicken nugget
16   smothered in ketchup?

17 MADISON: *(Jumps up.)* Then don't eat! Just don't eat! There!
18   That's my advice!

19 ZACH: Gee, thanks a lot! That really helped. See if I come back
20   to you for free advice again! *(Exits.) (MADISON takes a deep*
21   *breath and sits down. CARLY enters, rushing to the table in*
22   *a panic.)*

23 CARLY: I need some advice! I mean, I really, really, really need
24   some advice!

25 MADISON: Absolutely. Why don't you take a seat and we can
26   talk.

27 CARLY: OK. *(Sits down.)* So here's my problem. How do I get
28   Katlyn and Samantha to stop spreading rumors about
29   me?

30 MADISON: Well, first I suggest that you confront Katlyn and
31   Samantha ... in a very nice way of course, and ...

32 CARLY: *(Slams her hand on the table.)* Oh, I confronted them all
33   right! But it wasn't in a nice way!

34 MADISON: Then why don't you try it again, and this time ...

35 CARLY: And say what? "Katlyn, Samantha, would you please

1   stop spreading rumors about me?"

2   MADISON: Why don't you try a different approach and ask

3   them why they're spreading rumors about you.

4   CARLY: Oh, I know why they're doing it! It's because they hate

5   me!

6   MADISON: Then maybe you should ask them why they hate

7   you.

8   CARLY: Oh, I know why they hate me!

9   MADISON: Why? Why do they hate you?

10   CARLY: *(Flips hair.)* Because I'm cute.

11   MADISON: And they feel jealous?

12   CARLY: *Duh!*

13   MADISON: Well, maybe if you tried acting nice and ...

14   CARLY: I'm not acting nice to them!

15   MADISON: Then they could see that you want to be their

16   friend.

17   CARLY: But I don't want to be their friend! I just want them to

18   stop talking about me! So, what do I do?

19   MADISON: Ignore them.

20   CARLY: I'm not going to ignore them! But what I'd like to do ...

21   *(Punches fist in palm.)*

22   MADISON: No, no! You can't do that!

23   CARLY: Then what do I do? You're the one with all the free

24   advice here!

25   MADISON: Well, I say you invite them over to your house so the

26   three of you can talk.

27   CARLY: *(Punches fist into palm.)* Invite them over to my house?

28   No way! But I tell you what I am going to do!

29   REBECCA: *(Enters.)* I need some advice.

30   MADISON: I'll be right with you. *(To CARLY)* Your aggressive

31   behavior will only make things worse! Not to mention this

32   ... *(Punches fist in palm)* will get you expelled!

33   CARLY: Well, Katlyn and Samantha need to quit talking about

34   me!

35   MADISON: I still say that you either ignore them or try to make

1   friends with them.
2 CARLY: And that's stupid advice!
3 REBECCA: I know what I would do.
4 CARLY: What?
5 MADISON: I'll be with you in just a moment.
6 CARLY: What would you do?
7 REBECCA: I'd go to the principal's office. That way, Mr. Fry will
8   call the girls into his office and gripe them out!
9 CARLY: Yeah!
10 REBECCA: And if he hears about it happening again, they'll get
11   into big trouble!
12 CARLY: That's a great idea! Thanks! I'm going to the office right
13   now to talk to Mr. Fry. Thanks! *(Exits.)*
14 REBECCA: Hey, she liked my advice!
15 MADISON: *(Not happy)* And how may I help you?
16 REBECCA: You know ... never mind. I think I'll just take my
17   own advice on this one.
18 MADISON: Well, wouldn't you like my opinion?
19 REBECCA: I guess.
20 MADISON: So, what's the problem?
21 REBECCA: OK, the problem is that my mother won't let me
22   date.
23 MADISON: Ah ... the old, "too young to date" problem.
24 REBECCA: And I totally disagree.
25 MADISON: Of course you do.
26 REBECCA: All my friends date.
27 MADISON: All?
28 REBECCA: Well, most of them.
29 MADISON: And you think you're mature enough to handle
30   going out unsupervised with a person of the opposite sex?
31 REBECCA: Oh my gosh! You sound just like my mother!
32 MADISON: I'm just trying to get you to see both sides.
33 REBECCA: Well, I want my mom to see my side!
34 MADISON: Your side makes her nervous. She's worried about
35   your safety.

1 REBECCA: My safety? My boyfriend's not an ax murderer!

2 MADISON: Perhaps not, but he may not have the same morals
3   as you.

4 REBECCA: What does that have to do with going to see a movie?

5 MADISON: Well, you just never know!

6 REBECCA: Oh my gosh! I feel like I'm arguing with my mother!

7 MADISON: Would you like my advice?

8 REBECCA: No! But what is your advice?

9 MADISON: Listen to your mother. Realize that she has had
10   much more experience than you and she knows what's
11   best.

12 REBECCA: You know what?

13 MADISON: What?

14 REBECCA: Your advice stinks! *(Exits.)*

15 JOEY: *(Enters, sniffling.)* I need some advice.

16 MADISON: Of course. How may I help you?

17 JOEY: It's Katy ... *(Grabbing a tissue and sobbing)*

18 MADISON: And Katy is ... ?

19 JOEY: My girlfriend. No! Make that my ex-girlfriend!

20 MADISON: So your girlfriend just broke up with you? *(He nods,*
21   *unable to talk.)* And you're heartbroken? *(He nods.)* And
22   you feel like you can't go on without her? *(He nods.)* Have
23   you ever heard the saying, "Time heals"?

24 JOEY: What?

25 MADISON: It takes time. So right now, you need to embrace
26   your pain.

27 JOEY: What? Embrace my pain?

28 MADISON: Feel what you need to feel.

29 JOEY: Feel what I need to feel?

30 MADISON: Throw yourself down on the ground and cry if
31   needed!

32 JOEY: But I don't want to throw myself on the ground and cry!
33   I want to feel better! No! What I want to do is get her back!

34 MADISON: Are you speaking of revenge?

35 JOEY: No, no! Get her back as in her take me back!

1   MADISON: I see. Desperation.

2   JOEY: Yes, I'm desperate!

3   MADISON: Sending her a hundred text messages a day...

4   JOEY: Make that an hour.

5   MADISON: Begging.

6   JOEY: Pleading.

7   MADISON: Promising.

8   JOEY: I'll change! I'll do whatever!

9   MADISON: Has the stalking started yet?

10 JOEY: Stalking?

11 MADISON: Are you stalking her?

12 JOEY: No! Well, not much. *(Looks over his shoulder.)* I mean, I

13   know she's sitting over there with her friends. I mean, I'm

14   keeping an eye on her, but not stalking.

15 MADISON: Good, good. Because if you start stalking her, that's

16   when it becomes serious.

17 JOEY: So what do I do?

18 MADISON: Well, first, do you know why Katy dumped you?

19 JOEY: Because she needed space. Needed to breath. Needed a

20   break. All those things.

21 MADISON: Then you should give her just that.

22 JOEY: What? But I want her back!

23 MADISON: Begging and pleading will only have the opposite

24   effect. So, you need to embrace your pain and avoid her

25   completely.

26 JOEY: But I don't want to avoid her! I want to beg for her to take

27   me back! *(Gets on his knees.)* "Please, Katy, please! Please

28   take me back!"

29 MADISON: Won't work. I'm sorry.

30 JOEY: How do you know? Maybe if I offered her a bouquet of

31   flowers. *(Holds out his hands as if holding flowers.)* "Please,

32   Katy, please! Please take me back!"

33 MADISON: And are you willing to take the chance?

34 JOEY: The chance?

35 MADISON: The chance for more rejection?

1   JOEY: Of course I'm willing to take the chance! I dealt with it
2   between classes last period! Except I didn't have any
3   flowers. Yeah, right there in the hall, in the middle of the
4   students rushing to their classes, I dropped to my knees
5   and fell at her feet. "Please, Katy, please! Please take me
6   back!"
7   MADISON: What did she do?
8   JOEY: Yelled at me and walked away.
9   MADISON: I see. Listen, you really need to pull yourself
10   together.
11   JOEY: *(Stands.)* I can't.
12   MADISON: Think about having a little pride! You're too good
13   for Katy!
14   JOEY: I am?
15   MADISON: You are! And you're glad she broke up with you!
16   JOEY: I am?
17   MADISON: You are! And you wouldn't take her back if she
18   begged.
19   JOEY: Yes, I would!
20   MADISON: No, you wouldn't!
21   JOEY: OK. No, I wouldn't.
22   MADISON: It's a blessing in disguise.
23   JOEY: It is?
24   MADISON: It is! The tears are gone! The girl is gone! And you
25   couldn't be happier!
26   JOEY: *(After a pause, he grabs a Kleenex.)* You know what?
27   MADISON: What?
28   JOEY: Your advice stinks! And you know what else?!
29   MADISON: What?
30   JOEY: I'm going over to Katy's table right now and I'm going to
31   let her know how I feel!
32   MADISON: You'll be sorry.
33   JOEY: *(Pulls the poster off the table which reads "Free Advice".)*
34   And you need to change this!
35   MADISON: To what?

1   **JOEY: Lousy Advice!** *(Exiting)* **Katy! Katy! Can't we work this**

2   **out? Please take me back!**

3   **MADISON:** *(Stands.)* **I don't give lousy advice!** *(Replaces poster.)* **I**

4   **think my advice is good!**

28. Boys, Boys, Boys

CAST: (2F) SHERRY, BLANCA
PROPS: Notepads, pens.

1   *(At rise SHERRY and BLANCA are sitting at a table with*
2   *notepads and pens.)*
3   **SHERRY: We need a theme.**
4   **BLANCA: Boys!**
5   **SHERRY: We can't have boys as a theme.**
6   **BLANCA: Why not?**
7   **SHERRY: How would we do that?**
8   **BLANCA: We only invite boys to our party!**
9   **SHERRY: We can't do that.**
10   **BLANCA: Yes we can. It's our party.**
11   **SHERRY: Back to the theme. How about Mardi Gras?**
12   **BLANCA: Heather had a party like that a few months ago. Let's**
13   **do something different.**
14   **SHERRY: A Hawaiian Luau?**
15   **BLANCA: It's too cold for that.**
16   **SHERRY: Rock n' Roll?**
17   **BLANCA: Maybe.**
18   **SHERRY: Or the Wild, Wild West?**
19   **BLANCA: No, not that!**
20   **SHERRY: Well, you think of something.**
21   **BLANCA: I did!**
22   **SHERRY: Blanca, boys cannot be our theme.**
23   **BLANCA: It could be if we only invited boys.**
24   **SHERRY: My mother would not be happy if we only invited**
25   **boys.**
26   **BLANCA: Then let's invite more boys than girls. Because you**

1   **know at most parties we've been to, it's mostly girls that**
2   **show up.**
3 **SHERRY: Then we need to think of a theme that boys will like**
4   **so they'll show up.**
5 **BLANCA: That's true.**
6 **SHERRY: Football.**
7 **BLANCA: Yuck.**
8 **SHERRY: Basketball.**
9 **BLANCA: Double yuck.**
10 **SHERRY: Baseball.**
11 **BLANCA: Something besides sports.**
12 **SHERRY: Then you think of something, Blanca!**
13 **BLANCA: I already did! Boys!**
14 **SHERRY: And boys can't be our theme!**
15 **BLANCA: Food! Food can be our theme because boys love to eat!**
16 **SHERRY: Maybe, but we need to narrow it down.**
17 **BLANCA: OK. Give me some choices.**
18 **SHERRY: Italian, Chinese, American, Mexican, Barbecue ... ?**
19 **BLANCA: How about junk food?**
20 **SHERRY: Junk food?**
21 **BLANCA: Yeah! We can serve cookies, cake, chips, French fries,**
22   **donuts, hot dogs ... And we'll call it a Junk Food Party!**
23 **SHERRY: Well, I suppose ...**
24 **BLANCA: And who doesn't like junk food? I do! You do!**
25 **SHERRY: Well, I suppose boys would come to that.**
26 **BLANCA: Faster than they'd go to a Hawaiian Luau.**
27 **SHERRY: I guess we could do that. So, what about decorations?**
28 **BLANCA: Well, we could hang up pictures of junk food.**
29 **SHERRY: That sounds tacky.**
30 **BLANCA: Maybe, but we'll probably have the best turnout at**
31   **our party than anyone else has had all year!**
32 **SHERRY: You mean more boys.**
33 **BLANCA: Yeah! Do you remember how many boys showed up**
34   **for Desiree's party last weekend?**
35 **SHERRY: Three.**

1 BLANCA: And what was the theme? Let me remind you. Desiree
2   had a garden party where we sat around and drank tea out
3   of pretty little cups and stared at fake flowers. Now, was
4   that fun?
5 SHERRY: No. I don't even like tea.
6 BLANCA: And everyone left early, remember?
7 SHERRY: I couldn't wait. You're right. It would be more fun to
8   load up on chips and cookies.
9 BLANCA: And remember Natalie's tie-dye party?
10 SHERRY: That made me dizzy! All those bold, bright colors
11   everywhere.
12 BLANCA: And how many boys showed up?
13 SHERRY: Barney Cornish, III was there.
14 BLANCA: And how many boys was that?
15 SHERRY: One.
16 BLANCA: But at our party, there will be hundreds of boys! And
17   you and me.
18 SHERRY: Blanca, we have to invite some other girls, too.
19 BLANCA: How about all the girls from band?
20 SHERRY: Blanca, all the girls from band will be at marching
21   competition this weekend.
22 BLANCA: Oh, darn. Well, we tried.
23 SHERRY: Back to our guest list.
24 BLANCA: We'll invite all the cute boys from school!
25 SHERRY: *(Writing)* OK. Then Natalie, Desiree, Heather ...
26 BLANCA: My sister Kaci ...
27 SHERRY: *(Writing)* Kaci ... who else?
28 BLANCA: Gosh, I can't think of anyone else. Sounds like a good
29   list to me!
30 SHERRY: But ...
31 BLANCA: Perfect. A junk food party! With invitations to all the
32   cute boys from school, you, me, and four other girls, one of
33   which is my sister. This is going to be a great party!
34 SHERRY: *(Laughs.)* It does sound fun. Hey, let's go to the
35   computer and design our own invitations.

1   BLANCA: Yeah! And we can put pictures of all kinds of junk
2   food on the front. *(As they are exiting)* And let's invite Matt
3   and Kevin and Mitchell and Phillip and Cory and Ryan
4   and Donny and Jake and ...

29. The Pesky Fly

CAST: (3M, 2F) JERRY, JIM BOB, JAKE, CORRINA, LEANN
SETTING: School cafeteria.
PROPS: Food trays or lunch sacks.

1 (At rise JERRY and JIM BOB are eating lunch. JERRY notices
2 a fly and starts following it with his eyes as it moves in front
3 of him. After a minute, he begins waving his hand in the air
4 to shoo the fly away.)
5 JERRY: (Waving his arm in the air) **Go away!**
6 **JIM BOB: What?**
7 **JERRY: Get out of here!**
8 **JIM BOB: You want me to sit somewhere else?**
9 **JERRY:** (Slams his hand on the table.) **Darn! I missed! But I'll get**
10 **you next time!**
11 **JIM BOB: Are you talking to that fly?**
12 **JERRY: Who thinks he can share my lunch!**
13 **JIM BOB: Look, Jerry! He landed on my ...** (Points to his face.)
14 **JERRY: Don't move!** (Reeling his arm back)
15 **JIM BOB:** (Quickly moves.) **Whoa! You're not going to hit me in**
16 **the face!**
17 **JERRY: Hey, you moved!**
18 **JIM BOB: And if I hadn't, you would've hit me in the face?**
19 **JERRY: You would have been OK. And I wanted to kill that**
20 **pesky fly!**
21 **JIM BOB:** (Pointing) **There he is!** (They jump up, reach across the
22 table, and slam their hands down.)
23 **JERRY: Missed him again! Darn it!**
24 **JIM BOB: Maybe we scared him away.**
25 **JERRY: Maybe.** (Eating lunch) **He can just fly away and bother**
26 **someone else.**

1　JIM BOB: Yeah, like Corrina or Leann. 'Cause in English class,
2　　　they're always picking on me.
3　JERRY: Picking on you? Isn't that like elementary?
4　JIM BOB: Well, they act like they're in elementary! They're
5　　　always like, "Jim Bob, what's up with the shirt you're
6　　　wearing today? Jim Bob, have you ever heard of dressing
7　　　to impress?" Do you know what that means?
8　JERRY: *(Jumps across the table and slams his hand down.)* **Missed**
9　　　**again!**
10　JIM BOB: Do you dress to impress?
11　JERRY: Nah. I just wake up and throw on whatever.
12　JIM BOB: Me too! So what's wrong with what I'm wearing?
13　JERRY: *(Looks at him.)* Something's not right.
14　JIM BOB: *(Looking at him)* Are you serious?
15　JERRY: *(Slams hand on table.)* Serious.
16　JIM BOB: Well, can you narrow it down a bit for me?
17　JERRY: Look, Jim Bob, I'm no fashion guru.
18　JIM BOB: Maybe not, but you said I don't look right. So what
19　　　doesn't look right?
20　JERRY: *(Slams hand on table.)* Don't know. Ask Corrina or Leann.
21　JIM BOB: No! I'd never ask them!
22　JERRY: I'm sure they'd tell you what you're doing wrong.
23　JIM BOB: Oh, sure they would! They do that everyday! "Jim
24　　　Bob, why don't you let your hair grow out? Why don't you
25　　　brush it this way or that way? Have you ever considered
26　　　streaks?" Like, no! I'm not putting streaks in my hair!
27　JERRY: I don't think it's your hair. *(Slams hand on table.)*
28　JIM BOB: So what is it? My clothes? My hair? What? *(Stands.)*
29　　　Seriously, what is wrong with me?
30　JERRY: *(Stares at him.)* Don't move. *(Draws his arm back,*
31　　　*speaking slowly.)* Stand completely still.
32　JIM BOB: *(Quickly moves.)* Whoa! You're not hitting me!
33　JERRY: You moved! Look! There he goes! I could've got him!
34　JIM BOB: Hey, I know! Let's wait until he lands on *your*
35　　　forehead!

1   JERRY: Oh, he's not going to do that. He just wants to taunt me.

2   JIM BOB: Yeah, like Corrina and Leann taunt me! So seriously,
3   what's wrong with me?

4   JERRY: I told you, Jim Bob, I'm no fashion expert.

5   JIM BOB: But you said I didn't look right. Why?

6   JERRY: *(Stares at him for a moment, then starts looking above his*
7   *head, watching the fly. After a moment, he jumps onto the*
8   *chair and swats his hand in the air.)* **Leave, you pesky fly!**
9   *(Waving his arms in the air)* **Leave! Leave! Leave!**

10   JIM BOB: Is it my shirt?

11   JERRY: *(Looks at him.)* **Shirt looks OK.**

12   JIM BOB: My pants?

13   JERRY: They're just pants. How can you go wrong with a pair of
14   pants?

15   JIM BOB: I don't know, but obviously I got something wrong.
16   My shoes?

17   JERRY: Who cares what shoes you wear?

18   JIM BOB: Then what's wrong with me?!

19   JERRY: *(Throws his body across the table.)* **I got him!**

20   JIM BOB: Where?

21   JERRY: I'm on him!

22   JIM BOB: Are you sure?

23   JERRY: I think so.

24   JIM BOB: Maybe you squished him.

25   JERRY: Or he's trapped.

26   JIM BOB: What are you going to do?

27   JERRY: Lay here until he suffocates!

28   JIM BOB: Oh. Good idea. So, back to me ... *(CORRINA and*
29   *LEANN enter.)*

30   CORRINA: Jerry, what are you doing?

31   LEANN: Are you sick?

32   CORRINA: Or just acting stupid?

33   JIM BOB: He's killing a fly!

34   CORRINA: What?

35   LEANN: A fly? How are you killing a fly by lying on the table?

1 JIM BOB: He's suffocating him! *(Grabs his throat.)* He can't
2   breathe! He's gasping for air! He's dying ... dying ...
3 CORRINA: That's stupid.
4 JERRY: Hey, Jim Bob, don't you want to ask Corrina and Leann
5   a question?
6 JIM BOB: No!
7 JERRY: Yes, you do! Hey, Jim Bob wants to know what's wrong
8   with the way he looks.
9 LEANN: Jerry, why don't you tell him?
10 CORRINA: Since it's so obvious.
11 JERRY: Because I don't know what to tell him.
12 LEANN: Jim Bob, you just look ...
13 JIM BOB: What? What?
14 CORRINA: Weird.
15 JIM BOB: Weird? How do I look weird?
16 LEANN: You know, maybe it's not his clothes.
17 CORRINA: That's true.
18 JIM BOB: So my clothes are OK?
19 LEANN: Maybe we just thought it was your clothes.
20 CORRINA: And your hair.
21 LEANN: But maybe it's something else.
22 JIM BOB: What? What?
23 LEANN: It's just the whole ... you know ...
24 CORRINA: The whole person thing going on here.
25 JIM BOB: The whole person thing going on here? The whole
26   person thing going on here is me! So what's wrong with
27   me? Huh? Huh?
28 LEANN: Never mind.
29 JIM BOB: Never mind? You can't do that!
30 CORRINA: Jim Bob, you can't help what you look like.
31 LEANN: And maybe you'll grow out of it.
32 CORRINA: Like in ten or twenty years from now you'll be more
33   ... you know ...
34 JIM BOB: More what?
35 LEANN: Taller.

1 CORRINA: And you'll have a different hairstyle. If you're not
2   bald by then.
3 JIM BOB: Bald? I'm not going to be bald!
4 LEANN: You never know. My uncle Chester went bald in his
5   twenties.
6 CORRINA: Really?
7 LEANN: Really.
8 CORRINA: That's gross!
9 LEANN: I know.
10 CORRINA: I'd never date a bald guy. Unless he was shaving his
11   head to be cool. Then that'd be different.
12 LEANN: *(To JIM BOB)* Maybe you should shave your head.
13 CORRINA: Yeah!
14 JIM BOB: I'm not shaving my head!
15 CORRINA: And get a diamond stud in your ear. That'd be cute!
16 JIM BOB: It would?
17 LEANN: Yeah! *(Pointing)* Hey, Jerry, there's your fly.
18 JERRY: What?
19 LEANN: Right there on the table.
20 JERRY: *(Jumps up and leaps toward the fly.)* Come here you
21   pesky fly! I want you to die! Die, die, die!
22 CORRINA: *(Pointing)* There he goes.
23 JIM BOB: Shave my head and get a diamond stud? I don't think
24   my mom would let me do that.
25 JERRY: *(Jumps off the table and chases the fly around the room.)*
26   Come back! Come back here so I can smash your guts to
27   smithereens!
28 JIM BOB: You really think I'd look good if I shaved my head?
29 LEANN: Maybe.
30 CORRINA: You could always try it and see.
31 LEANN: And if not, well, it'll grow back. *(The GIRLS exit.)*
32 JIM BOB: *(Sits down at the table.)* Shave my head? I wonder ...
33 JERRY: *(Sits down at the table.)* I give up!
34 JIM BOB: Maybe you chased him away.
35 JERRY: Maybe. *(Pause as they continue to eat. After a moment,*

1 *JAKE enters with his lunch and sits down beside them.)*
2 **JAKE: Hey.**
3 **JIM BOB: Hey.**
4 **JERRY: Hey.**
5 **JAKE:** *(Looks over, then quickly slams his hand on the table.)* **Got**
6 **'em!**
7 **JIM BOB: You got him?**
8 **JAKE: Yep.**
9 **JERRY: But ... but ... That was my fly!**
10 **JIM BOB:** *(To JAKE)* **Not like his pet fly, but just the fly he was**
11 **trying to kill.**
12 **JAKE: He's dead now.**
13 **JERRY:** *(Slams his hand on the table.)* **But I wanted to kill him!**
14 **JAKE: Sorry.**
15 **JIM BOB: At least he's dead.** *(After a pause)* **I'm going to shave**
16 **my head!**
17 **JAKE: Cool.**
18 **JERRY:** *(Slams his hand down on the table.)* **Stupid fly!**

30. The Flower Delivery

CAST: (3F) CHRISTY, MELANIE, SHELBY
PROPS: Tissues.

1 CHRISTY: So here's the plan. I barge into fourth period to bring
2   you a flower delivery.
3 MELANIE: Which Jeff undoubtedly sees.
4 SHELBY: Oh, he'll be so jealous. And don't forget to act
5   surprised.
6 MELANIE: Oh, don't worry. I've been practicing that. How's
7   this? *(Acting surprised)*
8 SHELBY: And why don't you say something like, "Oh, he's so
9   sweet to do this!"
10 CHRISTY: Yeah, then dab your eyes with a tissue as if it's made
11   you cry.
12 MELANIE: That's a good idea.
13 SHELBY: And keep the bouquet in the center of your desk so
14   Jeff has to look at it the entire time.
15 CHRISTY: And keep smiling at the flowers as though you are in
16   love.
17 MELANIE: Oh, I can't wait to see his face!
18 SHELBY: And he'll never know the real story behind the
19   flowers.
20 CHRISTY: The set up.
21 SHELBY: The lie.
22 MELANIE: I sent them to myself.
23 SHELBY: We sure are lucky that Christy works in the office and
24   can deliver them.
25 CHRISTY: The flowers are hidden in the broom closet.

1 MELANIE: Did you remember the note?

2 CHRISTY: Yep. And I drew a huge red heart on the outside of

3   the envelope. Just so Jeff doesn't think you're getting

4   flowers 'cause someone died or something.

5 MELANIE: Good idea. But what if he leans over and asks me

6   who they're from?

7 SHELBY: Just say, "Someone."

8 CHRISTY: And be mysterious about it.

9 SHELBY: Or you could say, "Excuse me, Jeff, but you broke up

10   with me, remember? So I don't see how it's any of your

11   business."

12 MELANIE: Yeah, that's good. But what if ...

13 CHRISTY: What?

14 MELANIE: What if he sees my flower delivery and he shrugs as

15   if, "So ..."

16 SHELBY: Oh no, he'll be jealous! There's no way he can't be!

17   The two of you went out for almost three months!

18 MELANIE: And he's moved on.

19 CHRISTY: And so have you. Well, at least that's what he'll think.

20 MELANIE: I still don't understand how he could dump me for

21   Clarissa.

22 SHELBY: His mistake.

23 CHRISTY: His loss.

24 SHELBY: He'll be sorry.

25 CHRISTY: And jealous!

26 MELANIE: And maybe he'll want me back.

27 CHRISTY: Of course he will!

28 SHELBY: He'll beg to have you back by the end of the day.

29 MELANIE: But the question is, do I want him back?

30 CHRISTY: That's what all this is about, isn't it?

31 MELANIE: But maybe I don't want him back.

32 CHRISTY: That's fine. At least Jeff will know you've moved on.

33 SHELBY: And you're happy.

34 CHRISTY: And you have the most romantic new boyfriend

35   ever! A boyfriend who sends you a huge flower delivery

1   during fourth period!

2 MELANIE: But I don't have a new boyfriend!

3 CHRISTY: And who knows this?

4 SHELBY: Just the three of us.

5 MELANIE: So what's my new boyfriend's name?

6 CHRISTY: Does it matter?

7 SHELBY: She wants him to have a name, Christy.

8 CHRISTY: OK. So, what do you want your new boyfriend's

9   name to be?

10 MELANIE: Jeff.

11 CHRISTY: It can't be Jeff.

12 MELANIE: Why not?

13 SHELBY: Jeff Number two?

14 MELANIE: No.

15 CHRISTY: Jeff number one broke up with you and Jeff number

16   two doesn't exist so let's think of another name.

17 SHELBY: How about Tyler?

18 MELANIE: Yuck! No! Tyler sat next to me in kindergarten and

19   was so annoying!

20 CHRISTY: How about Jonah?

21 MELANIE: My cousin's name is Jonah. I'm not going out with him.

22 CHRISTY: It's just a pretend name.

23 MELANIE: Maybe so, but it needs to seem real.

24 SHELBY: How about Sid?

25 MELANIE: Sid has a million pimples on his face.

26 SHELBY: Not that Sid.

27 MELANIE: Well, that's what I think about when you say the

28   name Sid.

29 CHRISTY: Ryan?

30 MELANIE: Ryan is ugly.

31 SHELBY: Jerry?

32 MELANIE: Jerry, the class clown?

33 CHRISTY: Matthew?

34 MELANIE: Matthew is my brother's friend and I can't stand him.

35 SHELBY: Then you pick a name.

1 MELANIE: I did! Jeff.

2 CHRISTY: And Jeff is the boyfriend who dumped you, Melanie!

3   We need an imaginary boyfriend's name!

4 MELANIE: All I can think of is Jeff.

5 SHELBY: Well, maybe your imaginary boyfriend doesn't need a

6   name.

7 MELANIE: Yes, he does!

8 CHRISTY: Then I guess we'll have to go with Jeff two. The

9   flowers are from Jeff number two. Happy?

10 MELANIE: I wish they were really from Jeff.

11 SHELBY: Jeff number one?

12 MELANIE: Of course Jeff number one! Jeff number two doesn't

13   exist!

14 CHRISTY: So anyway, fourth period, you're sitting in class ...

15 MELANIE: Staring at the door.

16 CHRISTY: Don't stare at the door. It's supposed to be a surprise.

17   Then I enter Mr. Miller's class carrying this huge bouquet

18   of flowers ...

19 MELANIE: And I jump up and say, "Are those for me?"

20 SHELBY: Don't do that. That's too obvious. Just lean over to

21   someone in the class and say, "Gosh, I wonder who the

22   flowers are for?"

23 MELANIE: *(Repeating)* "Gosh, I wonder who the flowers are

24   for?"

25 CHRISTY: Then I will tell Mr. Miller that I have a special flower

26   delivery for Melanie.

27 MELANIE: From Jeff?

28 SHELBY: Don't say that! Say, "For me?"

29 MELANIE: *(Repeating)* For me?

30 CHRISTY: And then I'll bring them to your desk where you

31   smile and act surprised.

32 SHELBY: You can fake it, Melanie.

33 MELANIE: Oh, wow! Flowers! I wonder who they're from?

34 CHRISTY: And make sure Jeff sees the huge red heart on the

35   envelope.

1   MELANIE: What does it say inside the card?

2   CHRISTY: *(Smiling)* "From your imaginary boyfriend."

3   SHELBY: That's good, Christy!

4   MELANIE: I wish it were from Jeff.

5   CHRISTY: Why are you getting all depressed? You know Jeff

6   didn't send the flowers.

7   SHELBY: You're sending them to yourself!

8   MELANIE: And that's pathetic, isn't it?

9   CHRISTY: Not if it has a purpose.

10   SHELBY: To make Jeff jealous.

11   CHRISTY: To make him sorry.

12   SHELBY: To make him regret.

13   CHRISTY: And see that someone else wanted what he threw away.

14   MELANIE: But it's a lie! And how pathetic is it to send yourself

15   flowers because no one else will!

16   CHRISTY: You're overreacting.

17   SHELBY: I'd do it. That is, send flowers to myself.

18   MELANIE: You would?

19   SHELBY: Sure.

20   CHRISTY: Me too.

21   MELANIE: So it's not a dumb idea?

22   CHRISTY: No! It's brilliant!

23   SHELBY: I agree.

24   CHRISTY: It's all set. Fourth period you receive flowers.

25   SHELBY: And remember to act surprised.

26   MELANIE: *(Acting surprised)* Oh, I wonder who they're from?

27   *(As if looking at the card)* How sweet! Oh, he's just so sweet!

28   *(Dabs eyes.)* I think I'm going to cry! *(Begins crying.)*

29   SHELBY: Christy, I think she's really crying.

30   CHRISTY: She's just rehearsing.

31   SHELBY: No, really. I think she's crying.

32   CHRISTY: Melanie, are you crying?

33   MELANIE: Yes!

34   CHRISTY: Because you're so overwhelmed with the flower

35   delivery?

1 MELANIE: Yes!
2 SHELBY: Wow, she's good!
3 CHRISTY: Melanie, are those real tears?
4 MELANIE: Yes!
5 SHELBY: *(Hands her a tissue.)* Uh, Melanie, you might not want
6   to cry too much because then Jeff will think you're sad.
7 CHRISTY: And this is supposed to be a happy occasion.
8   Romantic. Touching. Heartfelt.
9 SHELBY: Why is she still crying?
10 CHRISTY: I don't know. Melanie, why are you still crying?
11 SHELBY: It appears that she's too upset to talk.
12 CHRISTY: But she's not supposed to be upset, she supposed to
13   be thrilled! Happy! Overtaken with joy.
14 SHELBY: I think she's overtaken with something else. Can't
15   you make her stop?
16 CHRISTY: What am I supposed to do?
17 SHELBY: I don't know. But do something.
18 CHRISTY: *(Suddenly)* Jeff isn't worth one single tear!
19 SHELBY: That's right! I wouldn't cry over him!
20 CHRISTY: Me neither!
21 SHELBY: *(After a short pause)* It's not working.
22 CHRISTY: I'd be happy to be rid of him!
23 SHELBY: Me too!
24 CHRISTY: And I wouldn't take him back if he begged!
25 SHELBY: Me neither!
26 CHRISTY: And he's ugly!
27 SHELBY: *(Gives Christy a strange look.)* He is? Oh! He is! He's
28   ugly!
29 CHRISTY: And he stinks!
30 SHELBY: Yes, he stinks!
31 CHRISTY: And ... and ...
32 SHELBY: *(Blurts.)* He's got another girlfriend!
33 CHRISTY: Shelby! *(MELANIE cries louder.)*
34 SHELBY: Who's ugly and stinks?
35 CHRISTY: Forget it, it's not working.

1   SHELBY: I'm sorry. I was trying.

2   CHRISTY: Melanie, pull yourself together by fourth period

3   because I am delivering that bouquet to you.

4   SHELBY: And remember to act surprised!

5   MELANIE: *(Suddenly, through her sobbing)* For me? I wonder

6   who they're from? *(Cries.)*

7   CHRISTY: *(Pulling SHELBY aside as they exit)* He's going to think

8   someone died.

9   SHELBY: I know. *(THEY exit.)*

10   MELANIE: *(Wiping tears)* For me? I wonder who they're from?

11   *(As if opening the card)* From my imaginary boyfriend!

12   *(Cries.)*

31. The Results

CAST: (2M, 4F) JADE, MEG, MATT,
DANNY, KRISTIN, DARLA

1   *(At rise JADE and MEG sit on the edge of an empty stage.)*
2   JADE: What part do you want?
3   MEG: What part do you want?
4   JADE: The main part, of course.
5   MEG: Me too.
6   JADE: *(Looks at her watch.)* Ten more minutes till Mr. Golden
7   posts the results.
8   MEG: He always leaves school the minute he puts up the list.
9   JADE: Probably because he doesn't want to see anyone being
10   disappointed.
11   MEG: Students crying.
12   JADE: Well, I'll cry if I get stuck with some stupid walk-on part.
13   MEG: And I'll cry if I get the part of the maid. Wouldn't that be
14   a terrible role? All dressed up in some ugly outfit, walking
15   on and off the stage carrying drinks and saying "Yes,
16   ma'am. Yes, sir. Will there be anything else?"
17   JADE: The part would be OK if she did something exciting in
18   the play. Like solving the crime or falling in love with
19   Professor Jenkins.
20   MEG. But she dies.
21   JADE: She's murdered.
22   MEG: I definitely don't want that part. Dead by the end of scene
23   one.
24   JADE: I don't want the part of the old woman, either.
25   MEG: I know! All bent over, carrying around a cane!
26   JADE: Not a part I'd be excited about having my friends and

1 family come watch me perform.

2 MEG: But the fair and beautiful Gweneth ... that's the part I

3 want!

4 JADE: Me too!

5 MEG: And if I get that part, maybe you'll get the part of my

6 sister! That'd be fun!

7 JADE: You mean the *ugly* sister?

8 MEG: We'd be in most of the scenes together.

9 JADE: Yes, and if *you* get the part of the ugly sister ...

10 MEG: I don't want that part!

11 JADE: Neither do I!

12 MEG: But if you get it?

13 JADE: I don't think that would happen. I honestly think I'll get

14 the part of Gweneth.

15 MEG: Well, so do I!

16 JADE: Well, only one of us can get that part.

17 MEG: Unless one of us gets to play Gweneth and the other gets

18 to be the understudy.

19 JADE: Who wants to do that? Memorize all the lines in hopes

20 the other person gets sick?

21 MEG: Well, we'd get to work together all the time. That'd be fun.

22 JADE: Would you be happy to just be the understudy for the fair

23 and beautiful Gweneth?

24 MEG: I want the part of Gweneth.

25 JADE: And so do I!

26 MEG: OK, let's say that you don't get the part of Gweneth and

27 the only female parts left are the maid who gets

28 murdered, the old woman with the cane, or a member of

29 the crowd. Who would you pick?

30 JADE: You know, Mr. Golden should have chosen a play with

31 more female parts.

32 MEG: I know. But who would you choose?

33 JADE: Between the maid, old woman, or part of the crowd?

34 MEG: Yeah.

35 JADE: Stage crew. What would you pick?

1 MEG: The same.

2 JADE: So I guess we're going for the same part. The lead actress
3   or keeping up with props.

4 MEG: Well, good luck.

5 JADE: Good luck to you, too. *(MATT and DANNY rush in.)*

6 MATT: Mr. Golden just posted the results!

7 MEG: He did?

8 JADE: Really?

9 DANNY: Just now!

10 MEG: Come on! Let's go look at the results! *(MEG and JADE rush*
11   *off.)*

12 MATT: They'll be disappointed.

13 DANNY: At least we weren't the ones to break the news to them.

14 MATT: Just call me Professor Jenkins!

15 DANNY: And I'll be the dark, evil visitor.

16 MATT: Who kills my maid!

17 DANNY: Sorry. But it's a great part.

18 MATT: They're both great parts. And we'll both be spending
19   plenty of stage time with the beautiful Gweneth.

20 DANNY: And not only is the character beautiful, but she's
21   beautiful in real life as well.

22 MATT: I've had a crush on her since first grade.

23 DANNY: I knew she'd get the part. No one else was suited for it.

24 MATT: Come on, you want to go practice our lines?

25 DANNY: Let's go. *(As they exit)*

26 MATT: "Welcome, Mr. Corbett! Your presence is unexpected but
27   welcomed."

28 DANNY: "Professor Jenkins, how might I express my gratitude
29   for allowing me to stay in your home?"

30 MATT: "No thanks is necessary, Mr. Corbett." *(They exit as*
31   *KRISTIN and DARLA enter.)*

32 KRISTIN: I can't believe I got the part of Gweneth!

33 DARLA: I can! You were great during tryouts.

34 KRISTIN: Thanks. So ... are you OK about your part?

35 DARLA: The maid? Sure! It'll be fun! I don't mind getting axed

1   in the first scene. That's less lines to memorize, plus the

2   rest of the play is about trying to solve my murder. So that

3   makes me very important.

4   KRISTIN: I like your attitude, Darla.

5   DARLA: Are you excited about the beautiful gowns you get to

6   wear?

7   KRISTIN: Oh yes! Those long, flowing dresses with sequins and

8   ribbons ...

9   DARLA: And you'll be ever so confused as Professor Jenkins

10   and Mr. Corbett fight for your love.

11   KRISTIN: *(Laughs.)* Well, only in the play. In real life ... *(Shakes*

12   *head.)* Never.

13   DARLA: But if you had to choose one?

14   KRISTIN: If I had to choose between Matt and Danny? You

15   mean in real life and not in the play?

16   DARLA: Just for fun. Who would you pick?

17   KRISTIN: And I have to pick one of them?

18   DARLA: Matt or Danny? Your choice.

19   KRISTIN: Like a happily ever after thing?

20   DARLA: Well, at least for the rest of the school year.

21   KRISTIN: *(Pause as she thinks.)* I think I'd rather be the maid

22   and exit after scene one.

23   DARLA: Chicken.

24   KRISTIN: They're good actors, but not my type.

25   DARLA: Come on, let's go run our lines. "Coffee or tea,

26   madam?"

27   KRISTIN: "Coffee, thank you."

28   DARLA: "Sugar? Cream?"

29   KRISTIN: "Yes, thank you." *(THEY exit. After a moment, JADE*

30   *and MEG enter.)*

31   JADE: At least we don't have to memorize lines.

32   MEG: No.

33   JADE: I think we get to act angry.

34   MEG: But most of the time we just stand around. Shall we

35   practice? *(A pause as they stand there.)* OK, we've got our

1   parts memorized.

2 JADE: Yep.

3 MEG: How hard is it to stand in the back of the stage? Oh wait!

4   We forgot to practice acting angry. You know, I don't think

5   I have to practice that emotion right now. Because I am

6   angry! Look! Look at me? *(Makes a mean face.)* How does

7   this look for being part of the angry crowd?

8 JADE: Good. But Meg, we get to be an understudy, too. I'm the

9   maid's understudy.

10 MEG: Who dies in scene one! And I'm the old woman's

11   understudy! Let's see ... why don't I practice that part!

12   *(Bends over as if using a cane.)* "Excuse me, dear ... excuse

13   me, can you help me? I'm trying to find the fair Gweneth

14   so I can hit her with my cane!"

15 JADE: Meg, she doesn't say that!

16 MEG: I know. But I was having a moment.

17 JADE: Kristin will be good as Gweneth.

18 MEG: I know.

19 JADE: Well, another good thing about being in the crowd is we

20   can stand in the back and have fun while Mr. Golden is

21   yelling at the actors to put more energy in their lines.

22 MEG: Or remember their lines.

23 JADE: And Phillip is in the crowd, too.

24 MEG: Oh yeah! Maybe I can stand next to him.

25 JADE: We're going to have fun. And I think Mr. Golden will see

26   how good we are at that and next year we'll get a leading

27   part.

28 MEG: Yeah, I hope so.

29 JADE: So let's practice.

30 MEG: Practice being in the crowd?

31 JADE: Yeah.

32 MEG: OK. *(A long pause as they stare straight ahead.)* Want to

33   practice the angry part now?

34 JADE: Sure. Let's try it. *(They make angry faces while raising*

35   *their fists in the air.)* Now let's practice the scene when the

1   **crowd watches Professor Jenkins give his speech.** *(Pause as*
2   *they stand there, expressionless.)*
3 **MEG: Well, I've got my part down. What about you?**
4 **JADE: Got it.**

About the Author

Laurie Allen was drawn to the theatre while performing plays under the legendary drama instructor, Jerry P. Worsham, at Snyder High School. In this small West Texas town, advancing to and winning the State UIL One-Act Competition in Austin was a goal often achieved. The drama department was hugely supported by the community and earned a reputation of respect and awe as they brought home many awards and first place trophies.

Following this experience, Laurie decided to try her hand at writing plays. Her first play, *Gutter Girl*, won the Indian River Players Festival of One-Act Plays Competition. With that, she was hooked, knowing she had found her place in the theatre. Now, more than twenty-five of her plays have been published by various publishing companies. Her plays have been performed at many theatres including The Gettysburg College, The Globe of the Great Southwest, The American Theatre of Actors, and the Paw Paw Village Players. Her plays for teens have enjoyed wide success with many going all the way to national speech and forensics competitions.

Laurie is currently working on her fourth book of plays for Meriwether Publishing Ltd., and on a full-length comedy play.

Order Form

Meriwether Publishing Ltd.
PO Box 7710
Colorado Springs, CO 80933-7710
Phone: 800-937-5297 Fax: 719-594-9916
Website: www.meriwether.com

Please send me the following books:

_____	**Comedy Scenes for Student Actors** **#BK-B308** by Laurie Allen *Short sketches for young performers*	$17.95
_____	**Sixty Comedy Duet Scenes for Teens** **#BK-B302** by Laurie Allen *Real-life situations for laughter*	$16.95
_____	**Thirty Short Comedy Plays for Teens** **#BK-B292** by Laurie Allen *Plays for a variety of cast sizes*	$16.95
_____	**Ten-Minute Plays for** **Middle School Performers #BK-B305** by Rebecca Young *Plays for a variety of cast sizes*	$17.95
_____	**Famous Fantasy Character Monologs** **#BK-B286** by Rebecca Young *Starring the Not-so-Wicked Witch and more*	$15.95
_____	**Improv Ideas #BK-B283** by Justine Jones and Mary Ann Kelley *A book of games and lists*	$22.95
_____	**112 Acting Games #BK-B277** by Gavin Levy *A comprehensive workbook of theatre games*	$17.95

These and other fine Meriwether Publishing books are available at
your local bookstore or direct from the publisher. Prices subject to
change without notice. Check our website or call for current prices.

Name: _____ e-mail: _____

Organization name: _____

Address: _____

City: _____ State: _____

Zip: _____ Phone: _____

❑ **Check enclosed**

❑ **Visa / MasterCard / Discover / Am. Express #** _____

Signature: _____

*Expiration
date:* _____ / _____

(required for credit card orders)

Colorado residents: Please add 3% sales tax.
Shipping: Include $3.95 for the first book and 75¢ for each additional book ordered.

❑ *Please send me a copy of your complete catalog of books and plays.*

Order Form

Meriwether Publishing Ltd.
PO Box 7710
Colorado Springs, CO 80933-7710
Phone: 800-937-5297 Fax: 719-594-9916
Website: www.meriwether.com

Please send me the following books:

_____	**Comedy Scenes for Student Actors** **#BK-B308** by Laurie Allen *Short sketches for young performers*	**$17.95**
_____	**Sixty Comedy Duet Scenes for Teens** **#BK-B302** by Laurie Allen *Real-life situations for laughter*	**$16.95**
_____	**Thirty Short Comedy Plays for Teens** **#BK-B292** by Laurie Allen *Plays for a variety of cast sizes*	**$16.95**
_____	**Ten-Minute Plays for** **Middle School Performers #BK-B305** by Rebecca Young *Plays for a variety of cast sizes*	**$17.95**
_____	**Famous Fantasy Character Monologs** **#BK-B286** by Rebecca Young *Starring the Not-so-Wicked Witch and more*	**$15.95**
_____	**Improv Ideas #BK-B283** by Justine Jones and Mary Ann Kelley *A book of games and lists*	**$22.95**
_____	**112 Acting Games #BK-B277** by Gavin Levy *A comprehensive workbook of theatre games*	**$17.95**

These and other fine Meriwether Publishing books are available at your local bookstore or direct from the publisher. Prices subject to change without notice. Check our website or call for current prices.

Name: _____ e-mail: _____

Organization name: _____

Address: _____

City: _____ State: _____

Zip: _____ Phone: _____

❑ **Check enclosed**

❑ **Visa / MasterCard / Discover / Am. Express #** _____

Signature: _____ *Expiration date:* _____ / _____
   (required for credit card orders)

Colorado residents: Please add 3% sales tax.
Shipping: Include $3.95 for the first book and 75¢ for each additional book ordered.

❑ *Please send me a copy of your complete catalog of books and plays.*